MOROCCAN ARABIC
PHRASEBOOK

D0009492

Dan Bacon
Bichr Andjar
Abdennabi Benchehda

Moroccan Arabic phrasebook
2nd edition

Published by
Lonely Planet Publications
Head Office: PO Box 617, Hawthorn, Vic 3122, Australia
Branches: 150 Linden Street, Oakland CA 94607, USA
10a Spring Place, London NW5 3BH, UK
1 rue du Dahomey, 75011 Paris, France

Printed by
Colorcraft Ltd, Hong Kong

Cover Illustration
Where's Abdul? by Chelle Rudelson

Published
February 1999

National Library of Australia Cataloguing in Publication Data

Moroccan Arabic phrasebook
2nd ed.
Includes index.
ISBN 0 86442 586 4.

© Lonely Planet Publications Pty Ltd, 1999
Cover Illustration © Chelle Rudelson

All rights reserved. No part of this publication may be reproduced, stored in a retrieval system or transmitted in any form by any means, electronic, mechanical, photocopying, recording or otherwise, except brief extracts for the purpose of review, without the written permission of the publisher and copyright owner.

About the Authors
Dan Bacon is an American who lived for eight years in Morocco where he started and managed Crown English Bookshop in the town of Agadir. Dan is currently employed as an engineer in the United States.

Bichr Andjar is a Moroccan who grew up and currently lives at Agadir, Morocco. He studied linguistics at the University of Agadir and has taught Moroccan Arabic to American Peace Corps Volunteers. Bichr is currently employed at the Airport in Agadir.

From the Authors
The authors wish to thank all of their friends in Agadir for their help in proofreading and making suggestions for the second edition of the phrasebook. Dan would like to thank his wife Kerry and sons Nate and Zach for their patience and understanding during the project.

From the Publisher
Vicki Webb co-edited the book, along with Justin Rudelson who provided linguistic expertise between fending off Australian wildlife. Peter D'Onghia proofread and kept a sanguine eye on production. Brendan Dempsey designed and laid out the book with the aid of Penelope Richardson, but didn't make the cast of Falcon Crest, and Chelle Rudelson created the cover and illustrations.

This second edition of the Lonely Planet Moroccan Arabic phrasebook was written by Dan Bacon and Bichr Andjar. Thanks to Abdennabi Benchehda who with Dan Bacon and Bichr Andjar wrote the first edition from which this book developed. The French and Berber chapters were compiled at Lonely Planet.

CONTENTS

INTRODUCTION

One of the first things you'll notice about Morocco is its linguistic diversity. French, Berber, Modern Standard Arabic, as well as Moroccan Arabic, can all be heard in the major cities, mainly due to the rich historical past of the country. The Berbers, the original inhabitants, make up roughly half of the population, and the three major dialects of their language are widely spoken. When the Arabs came to Morocco in the 8th century they brought their language, which has evolved into the Moroccan Arabic of today. France officially entered the picture in 1912 when it began the Moroccan protectorate and French is still widely used in commerce and the educational system.

When one speaks of Arabic in Morocco there are two languages to be considered. On the one hand there is Modern Standard Arabic. This is the direct descendant of the language of the Koran and is understood throughout the contemporary Arab world. In Morocco it's used in newspapers, correspondence, news broadcasts and speeches but rarely in conversation. Moroccan Arabic, on the other hand, is the first language of the majority of Moroccans and really the most useful language to know when travelling in the country. It differs from Modern Standard Arabic to the extent that non-Moroccan speakers of Arabic, with the possible exception of Algerians and Tunisians, find it difficult to understand.

Moroccan Arabic is strictly a spoken language and rarely written down. When it is written, the Modern Standard Arabic script is used and therefore has been adopted in this book. However, the script does reflect Moroccan Arabic pronunciation. It should prove useful to those who have had some previous exposure to Arabic as well as those wishing to make an attempt at learning the script. If you can't make yourself understood verbally, the script will be easily understood by Moroccans so you can point out the phrase you wish to communicate. Remember that Arabic script is read right to left starting from the top line.

This phrasebook has been designed to provide the language you'll need to survive as an independent traveller in Morocco, including Moroccan Arabic and basic introductions to French and Berber. It's also an invaluable complement to the guidebook, *Morocco*, published by Lonely Planet. Enjoy yourself and good luck!

ABBREVIATIONS USED IN THIS BOOK

adj	adjective
f	female
m	male
n	noun
pl	plural
sg	singular
v	verb

PRONUNCIATION

Most of the sounds in Moroccan Arabic are similar to English and correspond to the Roman letters used to represent them here. Sounds which don't correspond as closely to the Roman letters are explained in this chapter. Several of the Arabic sounds will be new to the native English speaker and difficult at first to produce. Take comfort in the knowledge that perfect pronunciation is not necessary for you to be understood and that Moroccans are quite patient and willing to help.

VOWELS

Short Vowels

a as the 'a' in 'at', very short
e as the 'a' in 'about', very short
i as the 'i' in 'hit'
u as the 'oo' in 'book'

Long Vowels

ā as the 'a' in 'father'
ī as the 'ee' in 'see'
ō as the 'oa' in boat
ū as the 'oo' in 'boot'

Diphthongs

ai as the 'y' in 'fly'
ow as the 'ow' in cow
ei as the 'ai' in 'wait'

CONSONANTS

Many Moroccan Arabic consonants are similar to those found in English, but there are some you should note. It might be useful to have a native speaker demonstrate these sounds.

g	pronounced as the ‘g’ in ‘go’, not as the ‘g’ in ‘gentle’
gh	a guttural ‘r’ approximated by gargling gently. Similar to the French ‘r’
H	similar to an English ‘h’, except pronounced deep in the throat with a loud raspy whisper. Try whispering ‘hey you’ loudly from as deep in the throat as possible
kh	similar to ‘gh’, except without the musical buzz from the voice box and similar to the ‘ch’ in German ‘bach’
q	similar to ‘k’, except pronounced further back in the throat
r	a trilled ‘r’ as in Spanish or Scottish
zh	as the ‘s’ in ‘pleasure’
‘	a glottal stop, as the sound heard between the vowels in ‘uh-oh’
ʿ	may be approximated by saying the ‘a’ in ‘fat’ with the tongue against the bottom of the mouth and from as deep in the throat as possible

Emphatic Consonants

The emphatic consonants ḍ, ṣ and ṭ are pronounced with greater muscular tension in the mouth and throat and with a raising of the back of the tongue towards the roof of the mouth. This sensation can be approximated by prolonging the ‘ll’ sound in pull.

The letters l, r, and z can occasionally be pronounced emphatically and are indicated in the book by a double consonant. Note in particular ‘God’, llah.

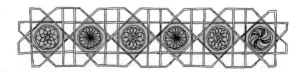

This chapter provides enough of the basics to get you communicating in Moroccan Arabic. Literal translations are provided when the word order of Arabic differs from English.

ARTICLES

In English the definite article is indicated by the word 'the'. The definite article in Moroccan Arabic is expressed in one of two ways, depending on the first sound of the word. If the first letter is b, f, g, h, k, m, ', q, gh, ḥ or ', then l is pronounced at the beginning of the word. If the word begins with d, ḍ, n, r, s, ṣ, sh, t, ṭ, z, **or** zh, then the initial letter is lengthened.

When making nouns and adjectives definite, the rule to follow is – if the first letter of the word is made with the tip or front part of the tongue then it is doubled. Otherwise place an l at the beginning.

bus	kar	the bus	lkar
paper/leaf	werqa	the paper/leaf	lwerqa
place	blāṣa	the place	lblāṣa
house	ḍar	the house	ḍḍar
street	zenqa	the street	zzenqa
price	taman	the price	ttaman

One unique feature of Moroccan Arabic is that the definite article is used with adjectives as well as nouns. See Adjectives and Building Sentences on pages 19 and 27 for examples.

ROOTS & PATTERNS

The concepts of 'roots' and 'patterns' are basic in understanding how Moroccan Arabic words are formed. Most words are built on a group of letters called roots. These roots are most often made up of three letters but can be four or, less frequently, two. The root appears with various vowels and consonants which make up patterns, and usually has some fundamental meaning that's modified by the pattern.

Here are two examples. The root ktb which always has a meaning associated with writing and ᶜlm is associated with information or learning:

kteb	he wrote
mektūb	written
ktab	book
ktūb	books
mektaba	bookshop
katība	secretary
mektab	office

ᶜlem	he was informed; he found out
ᶜallem	he taught
tᶜallem	he learned
taᶜlīm	education
mᶜallem	master in field or profession
muᶜallem	teacher

NOUNS

All nouns in Moroccan Arabic are either masculine or feminine. In general, nouns ending in a are feminine while those ending with any other letter are masculine.

Masculine		Feminine	
morning	sbah	food	makla
book	ktab	newspaper	zharīda
beach	bher	bed	namūsīya

Some exceptions include:

country	blad (f)	road/way	traiq (f)
hand	yedd (f)	sun	shemsh (f)
oil	zīt (f)	evening	msa (m)
ring	khatem (f)	water	lma (m)

Plural

Forming the plural of nouns in Moroccan Arabic is more complicated than in English. Each singular noun has its own plural form which is usually difficult to predict. The two most common ways of forming plurals are adding -īn to the end of masculine nouns and -at to feminine ones. There are many other patterns, so when learning words try to memorise the plural as well as the singular form.

Singular		Plural
hand	yedd	yeddīn
inspector	mūfetīsh	mūfetīshīn
bed	namūsīya	namūsīyat

PRONOUNS

Pronouns are divided into subject pronouns and object pronouns.

Subject Pronouns	
I	ana
you (m)	nta
you (f)	ntī
he/it	hūwa
she/it	hīya
we	hna
you (pl)	ntūma
they	hūma

Object Pronouns

me	-ī
you	-k
him/it	-ū
her/it	-ha
us	-na
you (pl)	-kum
them	-hum

Rather than appearing as separate words as in English, the object pronouns are attached to the end of other words in Moroccan Arabic.

he brought me	zhabī
he gave me	ʿṭānī
he brought him	zhabū
he brought her	zhabha
he brought them	zhabhum

Alternative forms of the object pronouns 'me' and 'him/it' are used when the final letter preceding the pronoun is a vowel.

to, for me	līīya
to, for him/it	līh

POSSESSIVE

Possession is most often expressed by the preposition dyal-followed by the appropriate object pronoun.

That shirt is mine.	dak llqamīzha dyaī (lit: that the-shirt belongs-to-me)
Her room is small.	lbīt dyalha sghīra (lit: the-room belonging-to-her small)

The possessives of certain nouns, particularly family members, are formed by attaching an object pronoun to the end of the noun.

friend	sahbū
her friend	sahbha
our friend	sahbna

Note that when the noun is feminine, the final a of the feminine noun changes to at:

mother	walīda
my mother	walīdatī
their mother	walīdathum

ADJECTIVES

Adjectives follow nouns in the sentence and must agree in gender and number. That is, if a noun is feminine and singular then the adjective that follows it must be feminine and singular as well.

Feminine and plural forms of adjectives are derived from the masculine base form. The feminine form of the adjective is formed simply by adding -a. The plural form of adjectives, as with nouns, is difficult to predict. The two most common patterns are adding -īn ('pretty', zwīn – zwīnīn) or replacing the long vowel sound in the middle of the word with a ('big', kbīr – kbar).

the small bed	nnamūsīya ṣṣghīra (lit: the-bed the-small)
the small beds	nnamūsīyat ssghar (lit: the-beds the-smalls)
He is big.	hūwa kbīr
She is tall.	hīya kbīra
They are tall.	hūma kbar

Comparative

The most common way of forming comparatives is to remove the long vowel from the regular adjective form (eg 'big' -kbīr, 'bigger' -kber).

He is bigger than my son.	hūwa kber men weldī (lit: he bigger than son-my)

VERBS

The following is an example of the way the present, past and future tenses are formed for the verb ktb , 'to write', in which all three letters of the root are consonants. Roots in which the middle or final letter is a vowel will differ slightly, but this should give a general idea of how the verb structure works. It isn't necessary to say the pronoun (I, we, you, etc) with the verb as it is in English. Every pronoun has a particular verb form, so it's clear from the verb alone who is performing the action.

ktb – 'to write'

Present Tense

I write, am writing	kan(kt)e(b)
you (m) write, are writing	kat(kt)e(b)
you (f) write, are writing	kat(k)e(tb)ī
he/it writes, is writing	kay(kt)e(b)
she/it writes, is writing	kat(kt)e(b)
we write, are writing	kan(k)e(tb)ū
you (pl) write, are writing	kat(k)e(tb)ū
they write, are writing	kay(k)e(tb)ū

Past Tense

I wrote	(kt)e(b)t
you wrote	(kt)e(b)tī
he/it wrote	(kt)e(b)
she/it wrote	(k)e(tb)at
we wrote	(kt)e(b)na
you (pl) wrote	(kt)e(b)tū
they wrote	(k)e(tb)ū

Future Tense

I will write	ghadī n(kt)e(b)
you (m) will write	ghadī t(kt)e(b)
you (f) will write	ghadī t(k)e(tb)ī
he/it will write	ghadī ī(kt)e(b)
she/it will write	ghadī t(kt)e(b)
we will write	ghadī n(k)e(tb)ū
you (pl) will write	ghadī t(k)e(tb)ū
they will write	ghadī ī(k)e(tb)ū

TO BE
Present tense
A verb usually isn't required when expressing 'to be' in the present tense, unless a re-occurring action is being described.

She's sick.	hīya mreiḍa (lit: she sick)
We are in Marrakesh.	hena felmerraksh (lit: we-are in-Marrakesh)
He's at the hospital on Mondays.	hūwa keikūn fessebīṭār nnhar letnīn (lit: he is at-the-hospital day on Mondays)

kan – 'to be'

I am	kankūn
you are	katkūn
he/it is	keikun
she/it is	katkuun
we are	kankūnū
you are (pl)	katūnū
they are	keikūnū

Expressing 'to be' in the past tense is similar to English except that it isn't necessary to use a pronoun.

Past Tense

I was	kunt
you were	kuntī
he/it was	kan
she/it was	kant
we were	kunna
you were (pl)	kuntū
they were	kanū

I was sick yesterday.	kunt mrīd lbareh (lit: I-was sick yesterday)
We were in Marrakesh last week.	kunna felmerraksh l'ūsbūʿ llī fat (lit: we-were in-Marrakesh the-week that-passed)

Future Tense

I will be	ghādī nkūn
you will be	ghādī tkūn
he/it will be	ghādī īkūn
she/it will be	ghādī tkūn
we will be	ghādī nkūnū
you (pl) will be	ghādī tkūnū
they will be	ghādī īkūnū

We are going to be in Marrakesh tomorrow.	hena ghādī nkūnu felmerraksh ghedda

There is/There are

kein (m)/keina (f)/keinīn (pl) are a special form of the verb 'to be', used to express 'there is/there are' in Moroccan Arabic. It's most commonly used with nouns, and agrees with the noun in gender and number.

There's a doctor in Marrakesh.	kein ṭṭōbeb felmerraksh
There are tomatoes at the *souq*.	lmaṭeisha keinīn fessūq
It's raining.	keina shshta (lit: there is rain)

GRAMMAR

KEY VERBS

to arrive	wsel
to be	kan
to bring	zhab
to come	zha
to cost	swa
to depart	ghrezh
to do	dar
to go	msha
to have	*See pp. 22–23.*
to know	ʿref
to live	ʿash
to make	dar
to meet	tlaqa
to need	htazh
to pay	ghelleṣ
to prefer	fḍel
to return	rzha
to say	gal
to stay	bqa
to take	ghad
to talk	tklem
to understand	fhem
to walk	temsha

TO HAVE

'To have' is expressed in Moroccan Arabic by the preposition ʿand, literally 'in the possession of', followed by an object pronoun.

I have	ʿandī
you have	ʿandek
he/it has	ʿandū
she/it has	ʿandha

we have	ʿandna
you have (pl)	ʿandkum
they have	ʿandhum
I have the ticket.	ʿandī lwurqa
They have the ticket.	ʿandhōm lwurqa
Do you have the ticket?	ʿandek lwurqa?

Expressing 'to have' in the past tense may seem confusing initially. It's accomplished by preceding ʿand- with the form of kan (see 'to be' past tense on page 20). ʿand- must match the subject of the sentence in gender and number and kan must match the object in gender and number.

I had the ticket.	kanet ʿandī lwurqa
I had the tickets.	kanū ʿandī lwūraq
He had the ticket.	kanet ʿandū lwurqa
He had the tickets.	kanū ʿandū lwūraq

MODALS

These are formed by placing two verbs next to each other in the sentence.

To Want

I want to go	bghīt nemshī
you want to go	bghītī temshī
he wants to go	bgha yemshī
she wants to go	bghat temshī
we want to go	bghīna nemshīw
you (pl) want to go	bghītū temshīw
they want to go	bghaw yemshīw

To Need

I need to go	khessnī nemshī
you need to go	khessek temshī
he needs to go	khessū yemshī
she needs to go	khessha temshī

we need to go	khessna nemshīw
you (pl) need to go	khesskum temshīw
they need to go	khesshum yemshīw

QUESTIONS

A statement can be made into a question by either changing your voice inflection, as in English, or by preceding the statement with wash.

This wallet is mine.	had lbeztām dyalī (lit: this the-wallet belonging-to-me)
Is this wallet mine?	wash had lbeztām dyalī? (lit: does this the-wallet belong-to-me)

Question Words

who	shkūn
what	ash
when	īmta
where	fīn
why	ʿlash
how	kīfash
whose	dyalmen
which	ashmen
how much	shhal

What's that?	ash dak shī? (lit: what that stuff)
When will it come?	īmta ghadī īzhī? (lit: when going it-come)
Where's the bank?	fīn lbānka? (lit: where the-bank)
How much is it?	shhal kayswa? (lit: how-much it-costs)

NEGATIVES

A sentence can be made negative by placing ma- at the beginning of the verb and -sh at the end of it.

He came on time.	zha felweqt (lit: he-came on-the-time)
He didn't come on time.	mazhash felweqt (lit: not-he-came on-the-time)

A sentence without a verb can be made negative by using mashī with an adjective.

The price is cheap.	ttaman rkhais (lit: the-price cheap)
The price is not cheap.	ttamam mashī rkhais (lit: the-price not cheap)

PREPOSITIONS

These prepositions don't occur separately but are fixed to the beginning of other words (eg 'the house' ddar, 'in the house' feddar).

with; by; by means of	b-/bī-
from; than	men-
between	bīn-/bīnat-
with	mʿa-
without	bla-
before	qbel-
in front of; facing	gôddam-
after	beʿd-
under; below	teht-
of; belonging to	d-/dyal-
behind	wra-
in; among	f-/fī-
on	ʿla-/ʿlī-
over; above	fuq-
next to	hda-
to; for	l-/lī-

CONJUNCTIONS

Conjunctions link things in a sentence. These things could be nouns, phrases or clauses.

or	awla
when/since	mnīn
in order to	bash
and	wô
if	īla/kūn
but	walakīn
until	hetta
even though	wakhkha
since	mellī

THIS & THAT

this	had
that (f)	dīk
that (m)	dak
those	dūk
this one (m)	hada
that one (m)	hadak
this one (f)	hadi
that one (f)	hadīk
these ones	hadū
those ones	hadūk
this thing/situation	had shī
that thing/situation	dak shī

this book	had lektab (lit: this the-book)
that girl	dīk lbent (lit: that the-girl)
That (one) is very good.	mezyan bezzaf hadak (lit: good very that one)

BUILDING YOUR OWN SENTENCES

As mentioned on page 20, the equivalent of the English verb 'to be' isn't normally required in Moroccan Arabic when speaking in the present tense. In this type of sentence the subject usually comes first.

I'm a teacher.	ana ʿūsted (lit: I teacher)
That man is at the hotel.	dak rrazhel felūtail (lit: that the-man at-the-hotel)

A simple sentence can be formed using a noun with the definite article followed by an adjective without the definite article.

The view is beautiful.	lmender zwīn (lit: the-view beautiful)
The bed is small.	nnamūsīya sghīra (lit: the-bed small)

Where a verb is present, the subject of a sentence can be placed either before or after the verb. Subject pronouns don't need to be stated as the subject can be understood by the form of the verb.

I went to the restaurant.	mshīt llmetʿam (lit: I-went to-the-restaurant)
The train left.	kherzhat lmashīna (lit: left the-train)

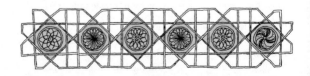

MEETING PEOPLE

Moroccans are legendary for their friendliness and hospitality. Most of them will be thrilled at your attempt to use their language and you'll have no trouble striking up conversations.

YOU SHOULD KNOW

Yes.	īyeh	ايه
No.	la	لا
OK.	wakha	وخة
Please.	ʿafak	عفاك
Thank you.	shukran	شكرا
	barak llāhū fīk	بارك الله في

Thank you very much.
shukran bezzef — شكرا بزاف

Without honour. (response to thank you)
bla zhmīl — بلا جميل

You're welcome.
(lit: You don't need to thank me for my duty.)
la shukran ʿla wezhb — لا شكرا علي واجب

Excuse me.
smeh līya — اسمح لي

No problem. (response to excuse me)
makein mūshkīl — ماكاين مشكل

GREETINGS & GOODBYES

When greeting Moroccans you'll find them more expressive than you might be accustomed to. One example of this is their liberal use of handshakes. Remember it's polite to shake each person's hand when entering a room or encountering a group of people. If this becomes unrealistic, pronouncing the phrase ssalamū ʿlekum is an acceptable substitute. Also notice that a handshake should be followed by placing your hand over your heart. It's common to greet close friends of the same sex by kissing them on both cheeks, especially if you haven't seen them recently.

The following phrases can be used when approaching someone you don't know. The first, ssalamū ʿlekum, is universal throughout the Arab world and appropriate for greeting both one person and groups.

Peace be upon you.	ssalamū ʿlekum	السلام عليكم
Good morning.	ṣbah lkhīr	صباح الخير
Good afternoon/evening.	mselkhīr	مساء الخير

The following phrases are less formal. They are spoken quickly, stringing several expressions together without necessarily waiting for a response.

How are you? (lit: No harm?)	labas?	لا باءس
How are you?	kīf halek?	كيف حالك؟
Fine, thank you.	labas, barak llāhū fīk	لا باءس بارك الله فيك
Is everything OK?	kulshī bekhīr?	كل شيء بخير؟
Fine, praise God.	bekhīr lhamdū llāh	بخير الحمد لله
What's happening?	'ash khbarek?	اش خبارك؟
How are you doing?	kī deir? (m)	كي داير؟
	kī deira? (f)	كي دايرة؟
	kī deirīn? (pl)	كي دايرين؟
Is your health OK?	ṣṣehha labas?	الصحة لا باءس؟
Is your family OK?	lʿa'īla labas?	العا ئلة لا باءس؟
Are your children OK?	ddrarī labas?	الدرارى لا باءس؟

The most common way to say goodbye is **bessalama**. Some other expressions to use when parting company are:

Goodbye. (lit: with peace)
  mʿa ssalama — مع السلامة
Goodbye. (lit: may God give you tranquility)
  lla yhennīk — الله يهنيك
May God help you. (to someone going to work)
  lla yʿuwn — الله يعون
Good night. (lit: may God grant you a good evening)
  lla yemsek ʿla khīr — الله يمسك علي خير
Take care of yourself.
  thella frāṣek — تهلاّ فراسك

CIVILITIES

Unlike English speakers who tend to improvise when polite remarks are expected, Moroccans draw from a large number of fixed expressions. The following are a few of the more common ones, along with the contexts in which they're used. Though not essential, these sayings will be appreciated when used correctly.

ensha'llāh — انشاء الله
  If God wills.
  (talking about the future or making plans)
tbarka llāh ʿlīk — تبارك الله عليك
  The blessing of God upon you.
  (complimenting someone on an accomplishment)
lla ybarek fīk — الله يبارك فيك
  May God bless you.
  (response to tbarka llāh ʿlīk)

lla ykhlef — الله يخلف
May God return it to you.
(after receiving hospitality or getting paid)

beṣṣāhhtek — بصحتك
To your health.
(to someone after a haircut or bath)

lla yʿṭeik sehha — الله يعطيك الصحة
May God give you health.
(response to beṣṣehhtek)

lla ysehhel — الله يسهل
May God make it easy for you.
(to a beggar when not giving anything)

lla yrhem waldīk — الله يرحم والدك
May God have mercy on your parents.
(when asking or thanking someone for help)

ʿla slamtek — علي سلامتك
Peace upon you.
(to someone arriving from a journey or recovering from an illness or calamity)

lla ysellemek — الله يسلمك
May God grant you peace.
(response to ʿla slamtek)

ṭṭreq ssalama — طريق السلامة
Have a peaceful trip.
(to someone leaving on a journey)

besmellāh — بسم الله
In the name of God.
(before eating, travelling or any activity you wish to do in God's name)

mbrūk! — مبروك!
Congratulations!

mrehba bīk ʿandna (sg) — مرحب بيك عندنا
mrehba bīkum ʿandna (pl) — مرحب بكم عندنا
You are welcome at our house.
(said to someone as they arrive to visit your home)

FORMS OF ADDRESS

When addressing men, asīdī, 'sir', is a polite title and one appropriate to use with men in official positions. When used before a name it is shortened to sī (egsī hamed). A common expression used to attract someone's attention on the street or when calling for the waiter in a cafe is shrīf. The expression sī muhamed can also be used in this way though it's not as polite. The frequently heard title hazh **(m)**/hazha (f) is ascribed to those who've made the Muslim pilgrimage to Mecca.

Alalla, equivalent to 'madam', can be used when getting the attention of a woman or when addressing her in conversation.

FIRST ENCOUNTERS

What's your name?
asmītek? اسميتك؟

My name is ...
smītī ... سميتى ...

His name is ...
smītū ... سميتو ...

Her name is ...
smīthā ... سميتة ...

I'm honoured to meet you.
metsherrfīn متشرفين

I'd like to introduce you to ...
bghīt nqeddemlek ... بغيت نقدم لك ...

MAKING CONVERSATION

Do you live here?
wesh katskūn henna? واش كتسكن هنا؟

Where do you live?
fīn katskūn? فين كتسكون؟

What are you doing?
'ash katdīr? اش كتدير؟

How long have you been here?
shehal mad wenta hna? شحل مد وانت هنا؟

I've been here for ...
mad ... wana hna — مد . . . وانا هنا

I'm going to stay for ...
ghadu nkless ... — غادو نكلس . . .

This is my first visit to Morocco.
hada marra lūla lūzhīt da lmaghreb — هد مرة لولة لوجيت د المغريب

Someone's waiting for me.
ktesstanna lī shi wahed — كيتستنا ني شي واحد

I've had a nice day.
hada lnhar kHabatnu — هد النهار كحباتنو

I'll call you on the phone.
ghadī nʿaytlīk ltelefun — غادي نعيطليك التليفون

I'm staying at ...
ana zhaless f ... — انا جالس ف . . .

I hope to see you again
knetsefa shūfak ʿud tānī — كنتصفا شوفك عود تاني

Where are you going?
fein ghādī? — فين غادي؟

Useful Phrases

Where are you going?	fīn ghāde?	فين غادي؟
Watch out!	ʿandak!	عنداك!
	balek!	بالك!
Be careful.	redd balek	ردّ بالك
It's clear/understood.	ṣāfī	صافي
Look!	shūf!	شوف!
Listen!	smaʿ!	سمع!
Not yet.	mazel bāqī	مازال باقي
Hurry up!	serbī!	سربي!
Slow down!	beshwīya ʿlīk!	ب شوية عليك!
I'm ready.	ana mūzhūd (m)	انا موجود
	ana mūzhūda (f)	انا موجودة
Go away!	sīr fhalek!	سير في حالك!
Leave me alone.	ʿṭeinī ttīsaʿ	عطيني التيساع
Leave us alone.	ʿṭeina ttīsaʿ	عطينا التيساع

I'll return in a little while.
ghadu nerzhaᶜ men daba madl shwey غادو نرجع من دابا ماد ل شوي
What do you think about ...?
'ash katfker fe ...? اش كتفكر ف ...؟
Is it OK if I take a photo of you?
wakhkha ntṣōwwerek? وخّا نتصورك؟
What do you call this?
'ash katsmīw hada (m)/hadī (f)? اش كتسميو هدّ/هدي؟
This is beautiful.
zwīn hada (m)/ zwīna hadī (f) زوين هدّ/ زوينة هدٍ
We like Morocco!
ᶜazhebatna lmaghrīb! عجباتنا المغريب!
That's amazing!
ᶜazhība! عجيبة!

I'm here on ...	zhīt l lmaghrīb fe ...	جيت ل المغريب ف ...
business	felkhedma	فل الخدمة
holiday	fel ᶜōṭla	فل عوطلة

Useful Phrases

Get away from me.	baᶜd mennī	بعد مني
What's the matter with you?	malek?	مالك؟
That doesn't interest me.	dakshī mayhemmnīsh	داك شي ميهمنيش
Yes I can.	īyeh nqder	ايه نقدر
No I can't.	la maqdersh	لا مقدرش
It's possible.	yemken	يمكن
It isn't possible.	mayemkensh	ما يمكنش
I forgot.	nset	نسيت
too much/a lot	bezzaf	بزّاف
a little	shwīya	شوية
important	mūhīm	مهم
not important	mashī mūhīm	ماشي مهم
very important	mūhīm bezzaf	مهم بزاف

NATIONALITIES

Where are you from?	mnīn nta? (m)	منين انت؟
	mnīn ntī? (f)	منين انت؟
	mnīn ntūma? (pl)	منين انتم؟
I'm from ...	ana men ...	انا من . . .
I live in ...	ana saken fe ...	انا ساكن في . . .
America	'amrīka	امريكا
Australia	ustralya	استراليا
Canada	kanada	كندا
England	anglatīra	انجلترا
France	fransa	فرنسا
Germany	almānya	المانيا
Italy	'īṭālīya	ايطاليا
Japan	el zhaban	اليابان
Morocco	lmaghrīb	المغرب
Netherlands	hulanda	هولاندا
Spain	īsbanya	اسبانيا
Sweden	sswīd	السويد
Switzerland	swīsra	سويسرا
the city	lmadīna	المدينة
the countryside	lbadīya	البادية
the mountains	lzhbel	الجبال
the suburbs of ...	ʿla berra men ...	علي البرا من . . .
I'm ...	ana ...	انا . . .
American	mīrīkanī (m)	مريكاني
	mīrīkanīya (f)	مريكانية
Australian	ustralī (m)	استرالي
	ustralīya (f)	استرالية
British	neglīzī (m)	نجليزي
	neglīzīya (f)	نجليزية
French	fransawī (m)	فرنساوي
	fransawīya (f)	فرنساوية
Italian	'īṭālī (m)	ايطالي
	'īṭālīya (f)	ايطالية

Japanese	lzhabanī (m)	ياباني
	lzhabanīya (f)	يابانية
Moroccan	maghrībī (m)	مغربي
	maghrībīya (f)	مغربية
Spanish	īsbānī (m)	اسباني
	īsbanīya (f)	اسبانية
Sweden	swīdī (m)	سويدي
	swīdīya (f)	سويدية
Swiss	swīsrī (m)	سويسري
	swīrīya (f)	سويسرية

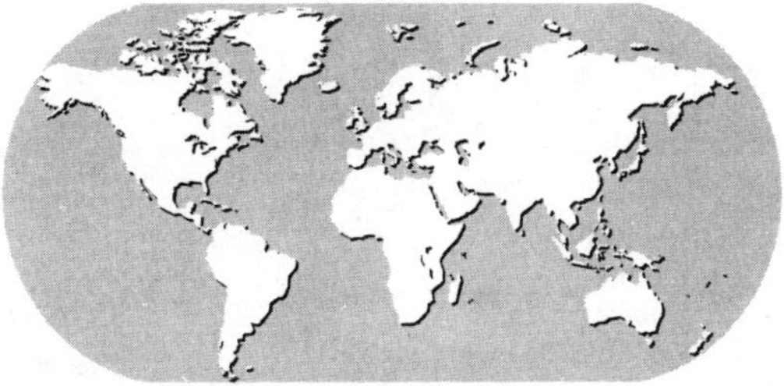

CULTURAL DIFFERENCES

How do you do this in your country?
kīfesh katdīrū hadshī felbladkum? — كيفاش كتديرو هد شي فل بلادكم؟

Is this a local custom?
wesh hadshī ʿadī felbladkum? — واش هد شي عادي فل بلادكو؟

This isn't the custom in my country.
hadshee mashī ʿadī felbladna — هد شي ما شي عادي فل بلادنا

I'm not accustomed to this.
ana mamwalfsh be hadsī — انا مامولفش ب هد شي

I'd like to watch but I don't want to join in.
bghiṭ nteferrezh walakīm mabghītsh ndekhul feha — بغيت نتفرج والاكن ما بغيتش ندخل فيها

AGE

How old are you?	shhal f'merek?	شحال ف عمرك؟
I'm ...	'andī ...	عندي ...
18 years old	tmenṭāshal 'am	تمنطاشل عام
25 years old	khamsa ū'shrīn 'am	خمسة و عشرين عام

Note: See the Numbers chapter for your particular age.

OCCUPATIONS

What's your occupation?

ash kat'amel? (m)	اش كتعمل ؟
ash kat'amlī? (f)	اش كتعملي ؟

I'm a(n) ...	ana ...	انا ...
businessperson	tazher (m)	تاجر
	tazhra(f)	تاجرة
carpenter	nazhzhar (m)	نجار
doctor	ṭbīb (m)	طبيب
	ṭbība (f)	طبيبة
engineer/architect	mūhendīs (m)	مهندس
	mūhendīsa (f)	مهندسة
government employee	mweḍḍef (m)	موظف
	mweḍḍefa (f)	موظفة
journalist	ṣāhāfī (m)	صحافي
	ṣāhāfīya (f)	صحافية
lawyer	mūhamī (m)	محامي
	mūhamīya (f)	محامية

retiree	qebt lantrīt (m/f)	قبطت لا نتريت
secretary	katīb (m)	كاتب
	katıba (f)	كاتبة
student	ṭāleb (m)	طالب
	ṭāleba (f)	طالبة
teacher	'ūstad (m)	استاذ
	'ūstada (f)	استاذة

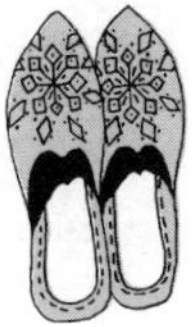

What are you studying?	ash katqrā?	اش كتقرأ؟
I'm studying ...	kanqrā ...	كنقرأ . . .
art	fenn	الفن
business	ltezhara	التجارة
education	ltalīm	التعليم
engineering	handassa	هنداسة
linguistics	lghāt	لغات
law	lHkūk	الحقوق
literature	lʿadāb	الاداب
medicine	ltebb	الطب
science	lʿūlūm	العولوم
math	lhessāb	الحساب
chemistry	kemyāʿ	كمياء
sociology	ʿūlūm ezhtemaʿya	علوم اجتماعية

RELIGION

What's your religion?
ashnū hūwa ddīn dyalek? اشنو هو دين ديالك؟

I'm ...	ana ...	انا . . .
Buddhist	būdī (m)	بودي
	būdīya (f)	بودية
Christian	masīhī (m)	مسيحي
	masīhīya (f)	مسيحية
Hindu	hendī (m)	هندي
	hendīya (f)	هندية
Jewish	īhūdī (m)	اهودي
	īhūdīya (f)	اهودية
Muslim	meslem (m)	مسلم
	meslema (f)	مسلمة

FEELINGS

I'm ...	ana ...	انا . . .
bored	meqnuṭ (m)	مقنوط
	meqnuṭā (f)	مقنوطة
happy	ferhan (m)	فرحان
	ferhana (f)	فرحانة
scared	kheif (m)	خايف
	kheifa (f)	خايفة
sick	mrīḍ (m)	مريض
	mrīḍā (f)	مريضة
tired	ʿeyyan (m)	عيان
	ʿeyyana (f)	عيانة
upset/angry	mqelleq (m)	مقلق
	mqellqa (f)	مقلقة
in a hurry	zerban (m)	زربان
	zerbana (f)	زربانة
worried	mqelleq (m)	مقلق
	mqelleqa (f)	مقلقة
sad	mqelleq (m)	مقلق
	mqelleqa (f)	مقلقة

I'm hungry.	fīya zhūwaʿ	فيّ جوعة
I'm thirsty.	fīya lʿaṭesh	فيّ العطش
I'm right.	ʿandī lhuqq	عندي الحق
I'm wrong.	mʿandīsh lhuqq	ما عنديش الحق

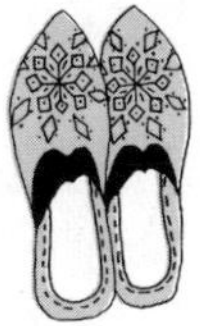

LANGUAGE DIFFICULTIES

I don't speak Arabic.
makanʿrefsh lʿarbīya — ما كنعرفش العربية

I only know a little Arabic.
kanʿref ghīr shī shwīya dyal lʿarbīya — كنعرف غير شي شوية ديال العربية

Do you speak English?
wash katʿref neglīzīya? — واش كتعرف نجليزية؟

Does anyone here speak English?
wash kein shī hedd henna lī keiʿref neglīzīya? — واش كاين شي حدّ هنا لي كيعرف نجليزية؟

I understand.
fhemt — فهمت

I don't understand.
mafhemtsh — ما فهمتش

Do you understand?
wash fhemtī? — واش فهمتي؟

What did you say?
ash gulltī? — اش كلتي؟

How do you say ... in Arabic?
kīfash katgūlū ... belʿarabīya? — كيفاش كتكولو ... ب العربية؟

What does this mean?
ash kat'anī hadhī? — اش كتعني هادي؟

Please speak slowly!
tkellem beshwīya 'afak! — تكلم بشوية عفاك!

Translate this word for me please.
terzhemlī had lkalma 'afak — ترجم لي هاد الكلمة عفاك

Write it down for me.
ktebha līya — كتبها لي

Please repeat it.
'awwedha 'afak — عودها عفاك

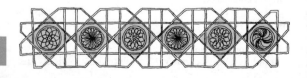

GETTING AROUND

Public transportation in Morocco is both inexpensive and easy to use. Within city limits, one can take either city buses or small (petit) taxis.

For trips between major cities, trains are the quickest and most comfortable means of travel, though they can be crowded at certain times of the year. The other options are buses and large (grand) taxis. The buses are the cheapest choice but can vary quite a bit in both speed and comfort. With grand taxis it is possible to pay on a per-seat basis as well as for the whole taxi.

FINDING YOUR WAY

I'm looking for ...
kanqelleb ʿla ... — كنقلت علي ...

How do I get to ...?
kīfesh ghādī nuwṣul l ...? — كفاش غادي نوصل ل ...؟

Is it near/far?
wash qrīb/bʿad? — واش قريب / بعيد ؟

Please show me on the map.
werri liya men l kharita ʿafak — وريني لي من الخريطة عفاك

Is there another way?
wesh kein shī trīq akhur? — واش كاين شي طريق اخر؟

Which way is best?
ashmen trīq hessen — اش من طريق حسن؟

Can we walk from here?
wash yemkin nzidu ʿla razhelīna? — واش يمكن نزيدو علي رجلينا؟

Where is the ...?	fīn kein ...?	فين كاين ...؟
city bus station	mheṭṭa dyal ṭṭōbīsat	المحطة ديال ال طوبسات
intercity bus station	mheṭṭa dyal lkīran	المحطة ديال الكيران
train station	lagār	لاكار
airport	lmāṭār	المطار
taxi stand	blāṣā dyal ṭṭāksīyat	البلاصة ديال التكسيات

Which ... is this?	ashmen ... hadī	اش من . . . هد؟
city	medīna	مدينة
street	zenqa	زنقة
boulevard	sharīᶜ	شارع

What time does the ... arrive/leave?

wufūqash keiwṣul/keikhrezh ...? (m)		وفكاش كيوصل / كيخرج . . .؟
wufūqash katwṣul/wkatkhrezh ...? (f)		وفكاش كتوصل / كتخرجي . . .؟
bus (city)	ṭṭubīs	الطوبيس
bus (intercity)	lkar	الكار
train	tran	تران
taxi	ṭṭāksī	الطاكسي
plane	ṭṭeiyyāra	الطيارة

DIRECTIONS

Go straight ahead!	sīr nīshan!	سير نيشان!
Turn right!	ḍōr ᶜal līmen!	ضور علي ليمن!
Turn left!	ḍōr ᶜal līser!	ضور علي ليسر!
Turn at the ...	ḍōr ...	ضور . . .
corner	felqent	ف القنت
traffic light	feḍō elhmer	ف ضو الاحمر
roundabout	ferrumpwan	ف الرمبوان
first street	fezzenqa llewla	ف الزنقة اللولة
second street	fezzenqa tteneya	ف الزنقة التانية
after	men bᶜd	من بعد
avenue	sharīya	شارع
behind	men lur	من اللور

between	ma bīn	مابين
corner	qent	قنت
far	bᶜeid	بعيد
in front of/opposite	quddem	قدام
near	qrīb	قريب
next to	hedda	حدا
slow down	beshwīya ᶜlīk	بشويا عليك
square	blāṣā	بلازا
stop light	ḍu lhmer	الضو الاحمر
stop sign	sṭup	ستب
street	zenqa	زنقة

Go backwards!
rzhaᶜ lur! رجع لورا!

Cross the street!
qtaᶜ ṭṭreq! قطع طريق!

Continue on a little further!
zīd qeddem wahed shwīya! زيد قدام واحد شويا!

How far? bshhal bᶜeid? بشحال بعيد ؟

north	shamel	الشمال
south	zhanūb	الجنوب
east	sherq	الشرق
west	gherb	الغرب

ADDRESSES

Moroccan addresses may be written in either French or classical Arabic. Written Arabic addresses usually take this format:

25 Mohammed V Boulevard
Rabat
25 shariᶜ muhamed lkhamīs ٢٥ شارع محمد الخامس
rbāt الرباط

BUYING TICKETS

I'd like a ... ticket to Casablanca please.	ʿafak bghīt wahed lwarka l ddar lbeiḍa ...	عفاك بغيت واحد الورقة ل لدار البيضة . . .
return	bash nemshī ū nzhī	نمشي و نجي
1st class	ddarazha llūla	الدرجة الاول
2nd class	ddarazha ttanīya	الدرجة الثانية

What's the fare?
shhal taman lwarka — شحال التمن ل ورقة؟

AIR

Air fares in Morocco are controlled by the national airline, Royal Air Maroc. It is the only company that offers internal flights and, while quite reasonable by international standards, is expensive compared to other forms of transportation. If you need to be somewhere in a hurry, air travel is worth checking out.

When is there a flight to ...?
'emta ghādī tkūn shī ṭeiyārāl ...? — امتي غادي تكون شي طيارة . . .؟

What time do I need to be at the airport?
'ashmen saʿa kheṣṣnī nkūn felmaṭār? — اش من ساعة خصني نكون ف المطار؟

Is it a direct flight?
wash rrihla direct? — واش الرحلة دريكت؟

How long is the flight?
sh hal dyal lwaqt ta ddir ltayara? — شحال ديال الوقت تدير الطيارة؟

Is the flight full?
wash ttiyarā ʿamra? — واش طيارة عامرة؟

domestic	mhalli	محلي
international	duwalli	دولي
arriving flights	lwusul	الوصول
departing flights	ddahab	الذهاب

I'd like to ... my reservation.	bghit ... hazhz dyali	بغيت ... حجزديالي
change	bdel	بدل
confirm	eked	آ كد
cancel	lghi	الغي

What's the charge for extra luggage?
shhal khes itkhelles ala lbagazh lli zayed? شحال خص اتخلص علي البكاج لي زايد؟

Is there a bus to the airport?
wash kain shi tubis lmatar? واش كاين شي طوبيس للمطار؟

Where can I catch a taxi to the airport?
fin khesni mshed taxi Lmatar? فين خصني مشد طاكسي ل مطار؟

I'd like to check in my luggage.
bghit nszhzhel l bagazh dyali بغيت نسجل البكاج ديالي

What's the flight number?
shhal rraqem dyal rrihla? شحال الرقم ديال الرحلة؟

My luggage hasn't arrived.
llbagazh dyali ma weselsh البكاج ديالي ما وصلش

BUS

local bus	ṭōbus	طوبيس
intercity bus	lkar	الكار

Give me two tickets to ... please.
qeṭṭaʿlī zhūzh dyal lwraq l ... ʿafak قطع لي جوج ديال الوراق ل ... عفاك

What time does the first/last bus leave?
wuqtash kaykhrezh lkar lewwel/lakher? وقتاش كيخرج الكاراللول / الاخر؟

Where's this bus going?
fīn ghādī had lkar? — فين غادي هد الكار؟

Is this bus going to ...?
wash had lkar ghādī l ...? — واش هد الكار غادي ل . . .؟

How much is it for a ticket from here to ...?
shhal katʿmel lwerqa bash nemshī men henna l ...? — شحال كتعمل الورقة باش نمشي من هنا ل . . .؟

Which bus is going to ...?
ashmen kar ghādī l ...? — اش من كار غادي ل . . .؟

Where can I catch a bus to ...?
fīn yemkenlī nqbed lkar l ...? — فين يمكن لي نكبد الكار ل . . .؟

When's the bus going to come?
'īmta ghādī izhī lkar? — امتي غادي ياجي الكار؟

How many buses per day go to ...?
shhal men kar kaymshī l ... fenhar? — شحال من كار كيمشي ل . . . ف نهار؟

Is ... far from here?
wash ... bʿeid men henna? — واش . . . بعيد من هنا؟

Is ... near here?
wash ... qrīb l henna? — واش . . . قريب لهنا؟

Please tell me when we arrive at ...
ʿafak īla wṣelna l ... gūlhalīya — عفاك الي وصلنا ل . . . كولهالي

Let me off here.
ōnzzelni henna — نزلني هنا

TRAIN

Where's the train station?
fīn kein lagār? — فين كاين لاكار؟

Is this train going to ...?
wash had ltran ghādi l ...? — واش هاد تران غادي ل . . .؟

Please give me two 1st/2nd class tickets.
ʿafak qeṭṭaʿlī zhūzh lweraq dyal dārāzha lewwla/tanīya — عفاك قطع لي جوج وراق ديال الدرجة الولي / الثانية

Is this seat free?
wash had lblāṣā khawīya? — واش هد البلاصة خاوية؟

This seat is taken.
had lblāṣāʿamra — هد البلاصة عامرة

Would you mind if I opened the window?
wash makein mūshkīl īla hlīt sserzhem? — واش مكين مشكل هليت سرجم؟

Where do I need to change trains?
fīn kheṣṣnī nbeḍḍel tran? — فين خصني نبدل تران؟

TAXI

Is there a taxi stand near here?
wash kein shī blāṣādyal ṭṭaksīat qrība l henna? — واش كاين شي بلاصة ديال الطاكسيات قريبة من هنا؟

How much for us to go to ...?
shhal khesna knkkhlsu hash nemshiiw? — شحال خصنا نخلصو باش نمشون ل . . .؟

I want to pay for one place only.
bghīt nkhelleṣ blāṣāwaheda — بغيت نخلص بلاصة وحدة

I want to travel with other people
bghīt nesafer mʿa nas khrin — بغيت نسافر مع ناس خرين

Do we need to pay extra for luggage?
wash khesna nekhlsu shi ziyada ala lbagazh? — واش خصنا نخلصو شي زيادة علي البكاج؟

Do you have change?
wash endak elserf ? — واش عندك الصرف؟

Go slowly please.
temsha bshwīya ʿafak — تمشي بشوي عفاك

Stop here please.
wqef henna ʿafak — وقف هنا عفاك
I'd like to get out here please.
bghīt nenzel henna ʿafak — بغيت ننزل هنا عفاك

Take me to ...	weṣṣelnī l ...	وصلني ل ...
this address	had lʿunwen	هدا العنوان
the airport	lmāṭār	المطار
the bank	lbānka	البنكة
I'm in a hurry.	ana zerban (m)	انا زربان
	ana zerbana (f)	انا زربانة
Please wait for me.	tsennanī ʿafak	تسناني عفاك
I'll be right back.	daba nzhī	داب نجي
Stop!	'ūqef!	وقف!

CAR

Where can I rent a car?
fin yimken li nekri shi tumubil tqa da liya lisans? — فين يمكن لي نكري شي طمبيل؟ تقضي لي لصانص
How much is it daily/weekly?
shhal ktaddir f luym/ssimana? — شحل كتدير فاليوم / صيمنة؟
Where's the next petrol station?
fin kayna shi bumba dyal lisans griba? — فين كاين شي بومبا ديال لصانص قريب؟
I'd like ... litres please.
bghit ... itru ʾafak — بغيت ... ايترو عفاك

Please check the ...	ʾafak shuf ...	عفاك شوف ...
oil	zzit	زيت
water	lma	الماء

Can I park here?
wash nqder nwakef hna? — واش نقدر نوقف هنا؟
How long can I park here?
sh hal men waket neqder nstatiun hna? — شحال من وقت نقدر نستشن هناالطاكسيات قريبة من هنا؟

air	hawa	هواء
battery	lbatri	الباتري
boulevard	sharīᶜ	شارع
brakes	lfranat	الفرنات
car	ṭōmubīl	طمبيل
clutch	vitas	فيتاس
dirt road	pīst	بيست
drivers licence	pirmi	برمي
engine	mutur	مطور
garage	lgarazh	الكراج
hire	kra	كرا
mechanic	mikanisyen	مكانيسيان
lights	dduw	ضو
oil	zzit	زيت
petrol	lïṣanṣ	ليسانص
puncture	pyasa	بيسة
radiator	rradyatur	رادياتور
map	lkharita	خريطة
seatbelt	smta	سمتة
speed limit	Hed suur'a	حد السرعة
tyres	pnawat	بنوات
windscreen	barbriz	بربريز

Car Problems

We need a mechanic.
khesna wahed lmikanisyan — خصنا واحد الميكانسيان

The car broke down at ...
tumubil khasra f ... — طمبيل خسرة في . . .

The battery is dead.
lbatri khawi — الباتيري خاوي

The radiator is leaking.
kayqtter rradyatur — كيقطر رادياتور

The car is overheating.
tumubil skhnat bezaf — طمبيل صخنت بزاف

I have a flat tyre.
ʾndi pyasa fruida — عندي بيسة فرويضة

It doesn't work.
ma khddamash — ما خدماش

I lost my keys.
ttudru liya swart — تضر لي سورت

BICYCLE

bicycle	beshklīṭ	بشكليت
motorcycle/moped	muṭur	مطور

Where can I hire a bicycle?
fin yimken li nkri bshklit? — فين يمكن لي نقري بشكليت ؟

How much is it for ...?	besh hal ghadi l ...?	بشحال غادي ل . . . ؟
an hour	saʾa	ساعة
the morning	lsabah	الصباح
the afternoon	lghita	الغيتة
the day	bel nhar	بالنهار

The tyre is flat. — ruida mghshuusha — رويضة مغشوشة

ACCOMMODATION

Hotels in Morocco are generally well furnished and reasonably priced. The majority are ranked using the European star system from one star (least expensive) to five star (most expensive). The prices of ranked hotels, except five star, are established by the government and are required by law to be posted. A list of all hotels and campsites is given out free of charge by the national tourist offices located in major cities.

When looking for accommodation you may be offered assistance by unofficial guides. Using a few Arabic phrases is a good way to let them know whether or not you need their services.

FINDING ACCOMMODATION

Where's a ...?	fīn kein ...?	فين كاين . . .؟
hotel	shī ūṭeil	شي اوطيل
Youth Hostel	'ūberzh, dār shshabab	اوبرج ، دارالشباب
campsite	shī mukheyyem	شي مخيم

I'm looking for a ... hotel.	kanqelleb ʿala shī ūṭeil ...	قنقلب علي شي اوطيل . . .
nice	mezyan	مزيان
clean	nqī	نقي
close	qrīb	قريب
cheap	rkheis	رخيص

What's the address?
ashnū hūwa lʿunwan? اشنو هو العنوان؟

Please write down the address.
kteb lʿunwan ʿafek اكتب لي العنوان عفاك

Please take me to a hotel.
weṣṣelnī l shī ūṭeil ʿafak وصلني ل شي اوطيل عفاك

I've already found a hotel.
ana lgīt shī 'ūṭeil baʿda انا لقيت شي اوطيل بعد

CHECKING IN

Is there a room available?		
wash kein shī bīt khawīya?		واش كاين شي بيت خاوي؟
I'd like to reserve a room.		
bghit uhzhez wahd lbit		بغيت احجز واحد البيت
What's the price of the room?		
shhal lttaman dyal lbīt?		شحل الثمن ديال البيت؟
Is breakfast included?		
wash lfṭur mhsūb mᶜa lbīt?		واش الفطور محسوب مع البيت؟
Which floor?		
ashmen ṭebqa?		اش من طبقة؟

I'd like a room ...	bghīt shī bīt ...	بغيت شي بيت . . .
for one person	dyal wahed	ديال واحد
for two people	dyal zhūzh	ديال جوج
with a bathroom	belhammam	بالحمام
with a shower	beddūsh	بالدوج
with hot water	belma skhūn	بالماء سخن
that's clean	īkūn nqī	اكون نقي
that's peaceful	īkūn trunkīl	اكون مهدن

I'll be arriving at ...		
ghādī nūwṣul fe ...		غادي نوصل ف . . .
Can I see the room?		
wash yemkenlī nshūf lbīt?		واش يمكن لي نشوف البيت؟
This room is good.		
had lbīt mezyana		هاد البيت مزيان
I don't like this room.		
maᶜazhbnīsh had lbīt		ما عجبنيش هاد البيت
This room is dirty.		
had lbīt mwessekh		هاد البيت موسخ

DID YOU KNOW ...

The word *kif* 'marijuana' is derived from Arabic *kayf*, meaning 'pleasure'.

Is there a room available which is ... than this one?	wash kein shī bīt ... men hadī?	واش كاين شي بيت . . . من هاد؟
bigger	kber	اكبر
smaller	ṣgher	اصغر
cheaper	rkheṣ	ارخص
better	hessen	حسن
cleaner	nqī	نقي

How much is a room for ...?	besh hal kein gbeit l ...?	بشحال كاين البيت ل . . .؟
one day	wahed nhar	واحد نهار
two days	yūmein	يومين
one week	wahed l'ūsbūʿ	واحد الاسبوع

I'm going to stay for ...
ghādī ngles ... غادي نجلس . . .

Is there hot water?
wash kein lma skhūn? واش كاين الماء سخن؟

Is there a safe where I can leave my valuables?
wash ʾendkum shi kufrfur nhut fih lhwayezh dyali lghalyeen? واش عندكم شي كوفرفور نحط فيه الحوايجديالي الغاليين؟

Should I pay now or later?
nkhelleṣ daba 'uwla men bʿad? نخلص دابا او لا من بعد؟

REQUESTS & QUERIES

Could we have an extra bed?
wash yemkenlek tzīdlīna wahed nnamūsīya? واش يمكنلك تزيدلينا واحد نموسية؟

Please bring me (a) ...	zhīblī ... ʿafak	جب لي . . . عفاك
towel	wahed lfuṭa	واحد الفوطة
blanket	wahed lbṭānīya	واحد البطانية
breakfast	lfṭur	الفطور
bottled water	qerʿa dyal lma	القرعة ديال الماء

ACCOMMODATION

Which room is ours?
ashmen bīt dyalna? — اش من بيت ديالنا؟
Please give me the room key.
ʿaṭienī ṣṣārūt dyal bīt ʿafak — عطيني ساروت ديال البيت عفاك
I've lost my room key.
tudder liya ssarut dyal lbit dyali — توضر لي ساروت ديال البيت ديالي

Where can I wash my clothes?
fin yemkenlī nṣebben hwayezhī? — فين يمكن لي نصبن حوايجي؟
Please clean the room now.
neḍḍeflī lbīt daba ʿafak — نضف لي البيت داب عفاك
Can I make a telephone call?
wash yemkenlī nʿmel telefun? — واش امكن لي نعمل تليفون؟
Do you change money here?
wash katserrfū lflus? — واش كتصرفو الفلوس؟

Can I leave a message?
wash nqder nkhlli shi wasaya? — واش نقدر نخلي شي وصاية؟
Is there a message for me?
wash kain shi wasaya dyali? — واش كاين شي وصاية ديالي؟
Please wake me at 7:00.
fiyaqni ʾafak f sabʾa — فيقني عفاك ف سبعة
Can I change to another room?
wash yemken li nthuwwel l bit akhar? — واش يمكن لي نتحول لبيت اخر؟

Please ... this for me.	ʿafak ... līya hada	عفاك . . . لي هادا
wash	ṣebben	صبن
iron	sleh	صلح
sew	kheyyeṭ	خيط

When will it be ready?
ʾemta ghādī tkūn mūzhūda? — امتي غادي تكون موجودة؟
I need it today/tomorrow.
ana mehtazh bīha lyūm/ghedda — انا محتاج بها اليوم/ غدا

I need it quickly.
ana zerban bīha — انا زربان بها

This isn't mine.
hadī mashī dyalī — هادي ماشي ديالي

Is the laundry ready?
wash lhwayezh wazhdīn? — واش الحوايج واجدين؟

COMPLAINTS

The ... doesn't work.	l ... khasser/ma khedemsh	ال...خاسر / ماخدامش
air-conditioning	lklimasyiun	لكليمايزيون
heating	shehd	شهد
electricity/lights	trisinti/duw	تريسيتي / الضو
key	ssarut	الساروت
shower	ddush	الحمام / الدوش
toilet	bit lma	بيت الماء
plumbing	taplumbit	تبلمبيت

Please fix it.
ʾafak suwebu/suwebha — عفاك صوبو / صوبها

Someone came into my room.
dkhel shīwahed felbīt dyalī — دخل شي واحد فالبيت ديالي

Something was stolen from my room.
tserreq shīhazha men bīt dyalī — تسرق شي حاجة من البيت ديالي

I'm locked out of my room.
tshed ʾliya lbab dyal lbit dyali men berra — تشد علي الباب ديال البيت ديالي من علي برا

This room is too ...	had lbīt ... bezzaf	هاد البيت . . . بزاف
hot	skhūn	سخون
cold	berḍ	بارد
loud	feha sḍaᶜ	فيها الصداع
expensive	ghalī	غالي

This ... is dirty	had ... mwessekh	هاد . . . موسخ
blanket	kashsha/bttaniya	البطانية / الكاشة
sheet	lizar	لزار
pillow case	lghassa dyal lmkhda	الغسة ديال المخدة
pillow	mkhdda/khddiya	المخدة / خدية

Please change it.
beḍḍelha ᶜafak — بدلها عفاك

The window won't open.
lsherzhem makeihelsh — الشرجم ما كيهلش

CHECKING OUT

We'd like to check out ...	bghīna nemshī ...	بغينا نمشي . . .
now	daba	داب
at noon	fettnash	ف الطناش
tomorrow	ghedda	غدا
tomorrow morning	gheḍḍa feṣṣbah	غدا ف الصباح

Please prepare the bill.
wezhedlīna lhsab ᶜafak — وجد لنا الحساب عفاك

Can I pay by ...?	wash yemkenlī nkhelleṣ b ...?	واش يمكن لي نخلص ب . . .؟
travellers cheque	shek sīyahī	الشيك السياحي
credit card	kārt krīdī	كارت كريدي

You made a mistake in the bill.
ghulṭō fel hsab — غلطو ف الحساب

I've already paid.
khulluṣt men qbel — خلصت من قبل

Can I leave my things here until this afternoon/evening?
wash yemkenlī nkhellī lhaweyzh dyalī henna hetta had lᶜshīya/illīl?
واش يمكن لي نخلي الحوايج ديالي هنا حتي هاد العشية / الليل؟

Call me a taxi please.
ᶜyyetlī ᶜla ṭṭāksī ᶜafak عيطلي علي طاكسي عفاك
Where's the laundry?
fīn keina shī meṣbana? فين كاينة شي مصبانة؟

Useful Words

address	ᶜunwan	عنوان
air-conditioning	klematīzasīyun	كليماتيزاسيون
arrival	wṣul	وصول
ashtray	tfeia	طفاية
balcony	balkun	البلكون
bathtub	hammam	حمام
bed	namūsīya	الناموسية
bedroom	bīt nnᶜas	بيت نعاس
blanket	bṭṭānīya	البطانية / الكاشة
chair	kūrsī	الكرسي
clean	nqī	نقي
cold	berd	برد
cost	taman	الثمن
crowded	zham	زحام
curtain	khamīya	الخامية
dinner	ᶜsha	العشاء
dirty	mwessekh	موسخ
door	bab	الباب
electricity	ḍō	الضو
empty	khawī	خاوي
food	makla	المكلة
full	ᶜamer	عامر

Useful Words

lift (n)	sensūr	سانسور
light bulb	būla	البولة
lock	qfel	القفل
mattress	mddreba	المضربة
mirror	mreiya	المراية
noise	ṣdaᶜ	صداع
pillow	mkhedda	مخدة
quiet	mhedden	مهدن
room	bīt	البيت
sheet	īzar	يزار
shower	dúzh	الدوش
sleep	naᶜsa	نعاس
soap	ṣābūn	صابون
spend the night	bat	بات
stairs	drūzh	دروج
suitcase	balīza	باليزة
table	tâbla	طابلة
toilet	bīt lma	بيت الماء
toilet paper	kaghit dyal bit lma	كاغيط ديال بيت الماء
towel	futa	فوطة
water	lma	الماء
window	sherzhem	السرجم

AROUND TOWN

LOOKING FOR ...

The quickest way to get oriented in a Moroccan city is to head directly for the local tourist office. They are normally located in the centre of town and offer free city maps which include the main municipal buildings and tourist sites.

When looking for a particular address you could run into trouble. Often streets and numbers are unmarked and many street names, especially in Casablanca and Rabat, have recently been changed from French to Arabic. The best bet is to ask a local shop owner if you suspect the address is nearby. If all else fails, the unofficial experts in giving directions are the small (petit) taxi drivers.

Where is a/the ...?	fīn kein ...?	فين كان ...؟
bank	shī bānka	شي بنكة
barber	shī hellaq	شي حلاق
bathroom	lbīt lma	البيت الماء
laundry	shī mṣebbana	شي مصبنة
market	lmarshei	المارشي
open air market	ssūq	السوق
old city	lmdīna lqdīma	المدينة القديمة
police station	lkūmīsarīya	الكوميسارية
post office	lbūsṭā	البوسطة
town hall	lbaladīya	البلدية
... embassy	ssīfara dyal ...	السفارة ديال ...
... consulate	lqunṣūlīya dyal ...	القنصلية ديال ...

How far is ...?
shhal bᶜeid ...? شحال بعيد؟
What time do they open?
weqtash keihellū? وقتاش كيحلو؟
What time do they close?
weqtash keiseddū? وقتاش كيسدو؟
Are they still open?
wash mazel halīn? واش مازال حالين؟

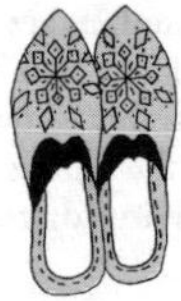

AT THE BANK

After bargaining for almost every purchase, you'll be pleased to find that currency exchange rates are fixed by the government and will be the same wherever you change money. Rates are posted, although a few banks have started charging a fee for changing travellers cheques.

Banking hours for most of the year are 8.30 to 11.30 am and 2.15 to 4.15 pm. During Ramadan (the Muslim month of fasting) and summer months, the hours change to 8.15 am to 1.45 pm. At other times, money can be changed at the international airports and most major hotels.

The dirham, Morocco's currency, cannot be exchanged once you're out of the country. Save your exchange receipts because you can change a percentage back into foreign currency at the airport when you leave.

I'd like to exchange some money.
bghīt nṣerref shī flūs بغيت نصرف شي فلوس
Has my money arrived yet?
wash weslu lflūs dyalī awla mazel? واش وصلو الفلوس اولا مزال؟

When will my money arrive?
’emta ghādī īwṣul lflūs dyalī? امتي غادي يوصلو الفلوس ديالي؟
Where should I sign?
fīn kheṣṣnī nweqqīʿ? فين خصني نوقع؟

Can I have money transferred here from my bank?
wash yemken llbanka dyalī واش يمكن للبنك ديالي
thawel shī flūs lhenna? تحول شي فلوس لهنا؟
How long will it take for the money to arrive?
shhal keikheṣṣ dyal شحال كيخص ديال الوقت
wekt lhqu lflus? الحكو الفلوس؟
I’d like to get some money with my credit card.
bhīt nakhūd shī flūs بغيت نخرج شي فلوس
belkart krīdī بالكارت كريدي

Useful Words

banknotes	wraq	وراق
cash window	ṣenḍuq	صندوق
change	ṣerf	صرف
money	flūs	فلوس
travellers cheque	shek sīyahī	الشيك السياحي

AT THE POST OFFICE

Stamps are available at tobacco stands as well as at the post office. It’s best to mail your letters at the mail slots outside post offices, as pick-ups can be infrequent at other mail boxes. Sending packages out of the country is fairly straightforward, although you’ll be asked to fill out a customs declaration form. Be sure to leave the package open because an official has to see the contents before it’s sealed.

I'd like to ...	bghīt ...	بغيت . . .
buy some stamps	nshrī shī tnaber	نشري شي تنابر
send a telegram	nṣeifeṭ wahed ttīlīgram	نصيفط واحد التليجرام
send a package	nṣeifet wahed lkūlīya	نصيفط واحد الكولية
send this registered mail	nṣeifeṭ hadī recūmāndei	نصيفط هد ركومندي

How much is it to send this to ...?
bshhal ghādī ... nṣeifeṭhadī l?
بشحال غادي . . . نصيفط هد ل؟

How much is it to send a postcard to the (USA)?
bshhal ghādī nṣeifeṭ wahed lkart pustāl l(amrīka)?
بشحال غادي نصيفط واحد الكارت بوسطال ل (المريك)؟

I want to send this by ...	bghīt nṣeifeṭ hadī ...	بغيت نصيفت هد . . .
air mail	beṭṭeiyyāra	بالطيارة
surface post	ʿadīya	عادية
express mail	bekspres	باكسبرس

Please give me a receipt.
ʿṭeinī fakṭura ʿafak
عطيني الفاكتورة عفاك

Has any mail come for me?
wash zhawlīya shī brāwat?
واش جاولي شي براوات؟

Useful Words

box	ṣenḍuq	الصندوق
breakable	ītherres	اتهرس
cardboard box	kartūna	الكارتونة
customs official	dīwānī	الديواني
envelope	zhwa	جوي
glue	lṣāq	لصاق
inspector	mūfettīsh	المفتش
insurance	lāṣurānṣ	لصورانص
mailman	faktur	فاكتور
number	raqem	رقم
pen	stīlū	الستيلو
phone stall in post office	bīt	بيت
stamp	tanber	التامبر
string	qennba	القنبة
tape	skātsh	السكتش
wrapping paper	kaghīt	كاغيط

TELECOMMUNICATIONS

For telephone calls, phone booths located throughout major cities are far and away the best choice. For anything other than local calls, they are much cheaper than hotels and always quicker than the post office. Reverse charge calls can be made either from a hotel or the phone section of the post office. State that you wish to call 'PCV' and provide your name as well as the name, city, country and number of the person you're calling.

I'd like to use the telephone please.
bghī nduwer ttelefūnʿafak — بغيت نضور التلفون عفاك

I want to call ...
bghit nʾeyyett ... — بغيت نعيط . . .

Here's the number.
ha raqem هاالرقم

How much per minute?
shhal ldqiqa? شحال ل دقيقة؟

I want to make a reverse charge phone call.
bghīt nʿmel ttelefūn PCV بغيت نضور التلفون ب س ف

It's busy.
mshghul مشغول

I've been cut off.
ttqtteʾ lkhett ʾliyya تقطع لخط علي

It's ringing.
tayserser تيسرسر

What's the area code for ...?
ashu huw landikatif dyal ...? اشو هو لندكتيف ديال . . .؟

Making a call

Hello. (answering a call)
allu الو

Who's calling?
shkūn? شكون؟

It's ...
hadā/hadī ... هدا/هدي . . .

Is ... there?
wash kain ...? واش كاين . . .؟

Yes, he's/she's here.
iyyeh, kain/kaina hna اية ، كاين/كاينة هنا

One moment.
wahed shwiyya — واحد شوي،
He/she isn't here.
makain/makainash hna — ماكاين / ماكايناش هنا
What time will he/she return?
imta gha yerzhe'/gha terzha'? — امتي غادي ارجع / ترجع؟
I want to leave a message.
bghit nkhlli wahd lmessazh — بغيت نخلي واحد المساج
Please tell her I called.
'afak gulleha rani hddert — عفاك كولها رني هضرت
I'll call back later.
ghadi b'ayet men ba'd — غادي بعيط من بعد

SIGHTSEEING

Where's the tourist office?
fin kain mktab dyal ssiyaha? — فين مكتب ديال السياحة؟
Do you have a local map?
wash kain 'andek lkharitta dyal mdina? — واش كاين عندك الخاريطة ديال المدينة؟

I'd like to see ...
bghit nshuf ... — بغيت نشوف . . .

cinema	lssinima	السينما
beach	bher	بحر
crowded	zham	زحام
market	l marshi	المارشي
mosque	zhzhame'	الجامع
parade	isti'rad	استعراض
park	'arsa	عرصة
university	lzhami'a	الجامعة

What's this building?
ash katkun had lbinaya? اش كتكون هد البناية؟

How much does it cost to get in?
shhal ttaman dyal ddekhla? شحال التمن ديال الدخلة؟

May I take a photograph?
wash yimken lli nākhud shi tssewwera? واش يمكن لي نخذ شي تصورة؟

I'll send you a photograph.
ghadi sʿfeit wahed tssewwera غادي صفت واحد تصورة

Please take a photograph of me.
swarni ʾafak صورني عفاك

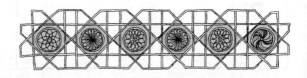

INTERESTS

COMMON INTERESTS

What do you do in your spare time?
'ash katdīr felweqt lfaragh dyalek? — اش كتديرفالوقت الفراغ ديالك؟

I like ...	kei'zhebnī ...	كيعجبني . . .
I don't like ...	makei'zhebnīsh ...	ماكيعجبنيش . . .
Do you like ...?	wash kat'zhebek ...?	واش كيعجبك . . .
art	lfin	الفن
cooking	ṭṭeyyeb	التطيب
dancing	shshṭīh	الشطيح
films	l'aflam	الافلام
music	lmūsīqa	الموسيقي
playing soccer	tl'ab kōra	تلعب الكرة
playing sports	tdīr rrīyada	دير الرياضة
reading books	tqra' lkūb	تقراء الكتب
shopping	ttessewuq	التسوق
travelling	tesafer	التسافر
watching TV	tferrezh fettelfaza	تفرج في تلفزة
writing	tekteb	تكتب

SPORT

Do you like to play sport?
wash kei'zebek tdīr rrīyada? — واش كيعجبك تدير الرياضة؟

I like playing sport.
'zīz 'līya ndīr rrīyada — عزيز علي ندير الرياضة

I prefer to watch, not play.
kanfeḍḍel ntferrezh ū manl'absh — كنفضل نتفرج و ما نلعبش

Do you play ...?
wash kat l'ab ...? — واش كتلعب . . .؟

Would you like to (play) ...?	wash bghītī tlᶜab ...?	واش بغيت تلعب . . . ؟
basketball	lbasket	الباسكيط
box	lbōks	البوكس
exercise	rrīyyaḍa	الوياضة
football	lkura	الكرة
hockey	lhōkī	الهوكي
rugby	rrōgbī	الركبي
ski	tzhlīq	تزحليق
surf	sserf	السورف
swim	ᶜōman	العومان
tennis	tīnnīs	التنيس

FAMILY

This is my ...	hada ... (m)	هدا . . .
	hadī ... (f)	هدي . . .
wife	mrātī	مراتي
husband	razhlī	راجلي
brother	khuya	خوي
sister	khutī	خوتي
mother	mmwī/lwalīda dyalī	امي / الوالدة ديالي
father	bba/lwalīd dyalī	با / الوالد ديالي
parents	waldīya	والدي
son	weldī	ولدي
daughter	bentī	بنتي
friend	ṣāhbī (m)	صاحبي
	ṣāhbtī (f)	صاحبتي

Are you married?
wash nta mzhūwzh? (m) — واش انت مزوج؟
was ntī mzhūwzha? (f) — واش انت مزوجة؟

I'm married.
ana mzhūwzh (m) — انا مزوج
ana mzhūwzha (f) — انا مزوجة

I'm not married.
ana mamzhūwzhsh (m) — انا ما مزوج
ana mamzhūwzhash (f) — انا ما مزوجة

Do you have any children?
wash ʿandek lūwlad? — واش عندك الولاد؟

I don't have any children.
mʿandīsh lūwlad — ماعنديش الولاد

How many children do you have?
shhal men weld ʿandek? — شحال من ولد عندك؟

I have ...	ʿandī ...	عندي . . .
one daughter	wahed lbent	واحد البنت
two daughters	zhūzh dyal lbnat	جوج بنات
one son	wahed lweld	واحد الولد
two sons	zhūzh dyal lūwlad	جوج ولاد

HOBBIES

Do you have any hobbies?
wash ʿandek shī hiwya? — واش عندك شي هواية؟

I like to ...	ʿazīz ʿalīya ...	عزيز علي . . .
cook	nṭeyyeb	نطيب
draw	nṣewwer	نصور
garden	lbastana	البستنة
sew	nkhīyyeṭ	نخيط
travel	nsafer	نسافر

I collect ...	kanzhmaʿ ...	كنجمع . . .
books	lktūb	الكتب
coins	ṣṣerf	صرف
stamps	ttnaber	تنابر

STAYING IN TOUCH

I'm leaving tomorrow.
ghadī nemshī ghedda — غادي نمشي غدا

Let's stay in touch.
khellīna ntshawfū — خلينا نتشاوفو

Let's swap addresses.
yallah ntbadlū lʿanawīn — يالاه نتبادلو العناوين

Do you have a pen and paper?
wash ʿandek stīlū ū werqa? — واش عندك ستيلو و ورقة؟

Here's my address.
ha lʿunwan dyalī — ها العنوان ديالي

What's your address?
ashnū lʿunwan dyalek? — اشنو العنوان ديالك؟

If you ever come to ... you're welcome at my house.
īla zhītī ... marhaba bīk f dārī — الي جيتي ... مرحب بك ف داري

Don't forget to write.
matnsash tkteb — ما تنساش تكتب

I'll send you copies of the pictures.
ghadī nṣefṭlek teṣṣawer — غادي نصيفت لك تصاور

It was great meeting you.
ana ferhan bash nʿarfek — انا فرحان باش نعارفك

SHOPPING

Morocco is a shopper's paradise. From exotic tribal jewellery to herbal cures, almost anything imaginable can be found in Morocco's markets (souqs). Every price is open for negotiation and bargaining is expected. Moroccan shop owners are known for their shrewdness so when haggling be prepared to match wits with some of the best. Using Arabic should allow you to not only have some fun but also get a better price.

LOOKING FOR

Where is a/an ...?	fīn kein ...?	فين كاين . . . ؟
bakery	fārrān	فران
barber	Hāllāk	حلاق
bookshop	shī mektaba	شي مكتبة
butcher	zhezzār	جزار
chemist/pharmacy	lfarmāsiyān	الفارماسيان
grocery shop	shī hanūt	شي حانوت
hardware shop	shī drūgrī	شي دروكري
laundry	māsbānā	مصبنة
open air market	ssūq	السوق
souvenir shop	bāzaar	بزار
tobacco shop	shī ṣṣakka	شي صاكة
travel agency	wekālet el āsfār	وكالة الاسفار
vegetable market	lmarshei	المارشي

Do you have ...?	wash ʿandkom ...?	واش عندكم . . . ؟
English newspapers	zhzhara'īd bneglīzīya	جرايد بنكليزية
film	lfīlm	الفيلم
a sheet of paper	wahed lwerqa	واحد الورقة
stamps	ttnaber	تنابر

Where can I buy ...?	fīn ghādī neshrī ...?	فين يمكن لي نشتري . . . ؟
soap	ṣṣābon	الصابون
maps	lkhārā'īt	الخرايط
pens	sstīlūwat	الستيلوات
pencils	lqlūma	القلوم

MAKING A PURCHASE

I'd like to buy ...
bghīt nshrī ... بغيت نشري . . .

Do you have anything else?
wash ʿandkom shī hazha akhora? واش عندكم شي حاجة اخري؟

I don't like it.
maʿzhebatnīsh ما عجبتنيش

Can I look at it?
wakhkha nshūfha? واش نقدر نشوفها؟

I'm only looking.
ghīr kanshūf غير كنشوف

How much is it?
bshhal? بشحال؟

Please write down the price.
kteb ttaman ʿafak — كتب التمن عفاك

Can I pay by credit card?
wash nkder nkhelleṣ bel kart kredī? — واش نقدر نخلص باكرت كريدي؟

Please wrap it.
zhmaʿha li ʿafak — جمعها لي عفاك

BARGAINING

Bargaining is an art in Morocco and is practised for almost every purchase. In fact, sellers will sometimes seem disappointed if you pay without an argument. To determine a fair starting price for an item in the souqs, you might try checking the same item at several different shops before zeroing in on the one you want. Depending on the item, offer an amount significantly below the price and see how quickly it drops.

The phrases below are most effective when said as if you're insulted the price is so high. Sometimes stomping away from the seller until he asks you to return also works. If you wish to maximise your bargaining position, avoid buying anything while you are with a 'guide'. They often receive a large percentage and thus inflate the prices.

How much?
bshhal? — بشحال؟

It's too much for me.
bezzaf ʿlīya — بزاف علي

That's very expensive.
ghalī bezzaf — غالي بزاف

Give me a reasonable price please.
dīr mʿaya wahed ttaman meʿqol ʿafak — دير معاي واحد التمن معقول عفاك

What's the last price?
akhīr taman shhal? — اخر تمن اشحال؟

That's my last price.
akhīr ttaman dyalī hūwa hada — اخر التمن ديالي هو هد

Is there one cheaper than this?
wash kein wahed rkheiṣ ʿla hada? واش كاين شي واحد رخيص علي هد؟

ESSENTIAL GROCERIES

Where can I find ...?	fīn ghādī nelqa ...?	فين نقدر نلق . . . ؟
I'd like to buy (a) ...	bghīt neshrī ...	بغيت نشري . . .
batteries	lḥāzhārāt	الحجرات
bread	lkhōbz	الخبز
butter	lzebdā	الزبدة
cheese	lfromāzh	الفرماج
chocolate	lchoklāt	الشكلاط
eggs	lbeyd	البيض
flour	dakīk	دكيك
gas cylinder	lbootā dyāl lghaz	البوطة ديال الغاز
honey	lʿāsāl	العسل
jam	kōfītīr	كوفيتير
laundry soap	lsāboon dyal tzbīn	الصابون ديال تصبين
margarine	marzharīn	مرجارين
matches	lwākd	لوقد
milk	lḥālīb	الحليب
olives	lzeitoon	الزيتون
pepper	lfleflā	الفلفلة
salt	lmelhā	الملحة
shampoo	shampwān	شمبوان
soap	lsāboon	الصابون
sugar	lsūkār	السكر

toilet paper	kāghīt	كاغيط
toothpaste	ldantifrīs	الدنتفريس
yoghurt	yōkort	يوكرت

SOUVENIRS & HANDICRAFTS

bag/purse	sak	صاك
basket	sella	سلة
blanket	bṭṭānīya	بطانية
brass	nhas ṣfer	النحاس الاصفر
carpet	zerbīya	الزربية
copper	lnhas lhmer	النحاس الحمر
cup/glass	lkas	الكاس
embroidery	ṭerz	طرز
leather	zheld	جلد
mirror	mraya	المراية
pitcher	ghorraf	غراف
plate	ṭebṣel	الطبسل
pottery	fekhkhar	الفخار
tray	ṣeinīya	الصينية
vase/pot	mhebbeq	المحبق

CLOTHING

Do you have one in my size?
wash ʿendeq shi wahed fltaqadda dyali? — واش عندك شي واحد ف التقد ديالي؟

Five in Your Eye

Depictions of the hand of Fatima (daughter of Mohammed) or the number 5, often found on jewellery, are believed to have the same effect as poking the fingers in the evil eye when used with the words khamsa fi ainek, 'five in your eye'.

Can I try it on?
wash neqder neshrbo? واش نقدر نجربو؟
It fits well.
zha mʿaya huwa hadak جا معاي هو هداك
It doesn't fit.
mashash mʿaya ما جاش معاي

It's too ...	hada ... bezzaf	هدا . . . بزاف
big	kbīr	كبير
small	ṣgheir	صغير
long	ṭwīl	طويل
short	qsīr	قصير
tight	mzīr	مزير
loose	translit	عريض

Do you have this in any other colours?
wash kein hada b shī lūn akhōr? واش كاين هد ب شي لون اخر؟
Can you alter this?
wash tqder thiyyid hāda? واش تقدر تحيد هد؟
When will it be ready?
'emta ghādī īkūn mūzhūd? امتي غادي اكون موجود؟

COLOURS

dark	meghlūq	مغلوق
light	meftūh	مفتوح
white	byeḍ	بيض
black	khel	كحل
blue	zreq	زرق
brown	qehwī	قهوي
green	khder	خضر
grey	rmadī	رمادي
red	hmer	حمر
yellow	ṣfer	صفر

boots	botīyon	بوطيون
bra	ssūtyīm	سوتيام
coat	lkbōt	الكبوط
dress	kswā	كسوة
hat	ṭerbūsh	الطربوش
jacket	kebboṭ	كبوط
pants	serwal	السروال
shirt	lqamīzha	القميجة
shoes	lṣebbaṭ	الصباط
socks	tqasher	تقاشر
sports shoes	ṣberdīla	سبرديلا
sweater	trīkū	تريكو
swimsuit	hwayezh d lʿumān	حوايج دالعومان
T-shirt	tīshūrt	تي شورت
umbrella	lmddel	المضل
underwear	slīp	السليب

TOILETRIES

after-shave/perfume	rīha	الريحة
deodorant	dyodoron	ديودرون
razor	zezwar	الزيزوار
shampoo	shampwan	شمبوان
soap	ṣābōn	الصابون
sun block	lomber	لمبر
tampons	fota dyal dem lhīd	فوطة ديال دم الحيض
toothbrush	shīṭa dyal ssnan	الشيتة ديال السنان
toothpaste	mʿzhūn dyal ssnan	معجون ديال سنان
toilet paper	kaghīt dyal bīt lma	كغيط ديال بيت الماء

FOR THE BABY

baby food	makla dyal drrī sghīr	مكلة ديال دري صغير
baby powder	ttalk	الطالك
bib	ryaka	الرياكة
disposable nappies	lkhrūk	الخروق
dummy/pacifier	lskāta	السكاتة
feeding bottle	lrdda'ā	الرضاعة
nappy/diaper	lkhrūq	الخروق
nappy rash cream	lpomād	البوماد
powdered milk	Hlīb dyāl lghbrā	الحليب ديال الغبرة
formula	farina dyāl drarī sghār	فرينة ديال دراري صغار

STATIONERY & PUBLICATIONS

Is there an English language bookshop here?
wash kayna shī mktaba dyal nglīziya hna?
واش كاين شي مكتبة ديال نكليزية هنا؟

Do you have an English language section?
wash 'endkom lktūb dyal lngliziya?
واش عنكم الكتوب ديال النكليزية؟

Do you sell ...?	wash katbī'ū ...?	واش كتبيعو . . . ؟
books	lektub	الكتب
magazines	lmazhellat	المجلات
newspapers	zhzhara'īd	الجرايد
paper	lwurak	الوراق

postcards	lekart postal	لكارت بوسطال
envelopes	zhzhwa	جوي
stamps	ttnaber	التنابر
pens	sstīlowat	ستيلوات
pencils	leqlam	القلام
city maps	lkhrayet dyal lmdina	خرايط ديال المدينة
road maps	lkhrayet dyal trqan	خرايط ديال طرقان

MUSIC

I'm looking for a ...	kanqelleb ʿla ...	كنقلب علي . . .
CD	dīsk llazer	ديسك لايزر
cassette tape	kasīt dyal lmūsazhela	كسط ديال المسجلة

traditional	teqlīdī	تقليدي
modern	ʿessrī	عصري

Please recommend some Moroccan music.
ʿafak khtar li shi mūsika maghrebīya
عفاك ختارلي شي موسيقي مغربية

Do you have any ...? wash ʿendek shi ...? واش عندك شي . . . ؟

Can I listen to this here?
wash yimken lī nsmeʿ lhadī hna? واش يمكن لي نسمع ل هد هنا؟

I need a blank tape.
khsnī kassīt khawiya خصني كسيط خاوية

PHOTOGRAPHY

How much is it to process this film?
bshhāl tHmīd dyal hada lfilm? بشحال تحميض ديال هد الفيلم؟

When will it be ready?
imta ghadī ykūn mwezhūd? امتي غادي يكون موجود؟

I'd like a film for this camera please.
bghīt wahed lfīlm lhad sssawara ʿafak بغيت واحد الفيلم لهد صورة عفاك

Can you install this film please?
wash tqder tweshshed liya had lfīlm ʿafak? واش تقدر توجد لي هد الفيلم عفاك؟

I'd like some passport photos please.
bghīt shī tsawer dyāl lpaspor ʿafak بغيت شي تصاور ديال البسبورت عفاك

My camera doesn't work.
sūra dyali khāsrā صورة ديالي خاسرة

The film is jammed.
lfīlm khser الفيلم خسر

The battery is dead.
lHzhrā mmiyta الحجرة ميتة

Do you have a battery for this camera?
wash ʿendek shī hzhra dyal had ssowara? واش عندك شي حجرة ديال هد صورة؟

battery	Hzhrā	حجرة
black & white	lbyīd ū lkhel	البيض و الكحل
colour	llūn	اللون
film	film	فيلم
film speed	surʿet lfīlm	سرعة الفيلم
flash	flāsh	فلاش
lens	zhzhazhat	ججات
video tape	kassīt vī dyo	كاصيط فيديو

WEIGHTS & MEASURES

gram	gram	كرام
kilogram	kīlū	كيلو
metre	mītrū	ميترو
centimetre	ṣāntīm	سنتيم
litre	lītro	ليترو
half a litre	ness leetro	نص ليترو
a little bit	shī shwīya	شي شوية

SIZES & COMPARISONS

big	kbīr	كبير
bigger than this	kber men hada	كبر من هدا
too big for me	kbīr ʿlīya	كبير علي
small	ṣghīr	صغير
smaller than this	ṣgher men hada	صغير من هد
too small for me	ṣghīr ʿlīya	صغير علي
tight	mzeyyer	مزير
long	ṭwīl	طويل
many/a lot/too much	bezzaf	بزاف

Polite Forms of Address

Polite forms of address, roughly equivalent to Mr, Mrs and Ms are sī, asīdī and alalla, followed by a first name. In return you may be addressed as 'Mr Max' or 'Mrs Sandra'.

a little bit	shwīya	شوي
enough	baraka	بارك
like/the same	bhal bhal	بحال بحال
heavy	tqīl	تقيل
light	khfīf	خفيف

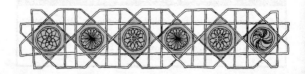

FOOD

MOROCCAN HOSPITALITY

One of the most important ingredients of the national cuisine is the gracious and hospitable atmosphere of the Moroccan home. If you're invited for a meal, here are some things to keep in mind. First, shoes are not normally worn inside so you'll be expected to remove yours before stepping on any carpets. Don't worry about washing your hands, your host will bring a basin with water to you while you're seated.

Once the host pronounces besmīllah, 'in the name of God', the meal will begin with everyone eating out of a common dish with their hands or, if kūskūs is served, possibly with spoons. The meat will be in the centre of the dish under vegetables and is eaten last, often being divided and distributed by the host. Don't eat too much because what often appears to be the main course will actually be the first of two or three! Be ready for some strong encouragement to continue eating even after you're full – your host wants to make sure you feel welcome. The phrase llah yzhʿa lbaraka, 'may God bring (you) a blessing', is a polite way of saying you've had enough.

MEALS

We would like to have ...	bghīna ...	بغينا . . .
breakfast	nfeṭru	نفطرو
lunch	nteghddaw	نتغداو
dinner	ntʿshaw	نتعشو

VEGETARIAN & SPECIAL MEALS

I don't eat meat.
makanakūlsh lhem — انا ماكنكولش اللحم

I don't eat chicken, fish or pork.
makanakūlsh dzhazh, lhōt awla hlūf — ماكنكولش ادجاج لا الحوت ولا الحلوف

I don't eat dairy products.
makanakūlsh makla lī fīhā halīb — ماكنكولش مكلة لي فيها الحليب

Do you have anything without meat?
wash kein shī hazha bla lham? — واش كاين شي حاجة بلا اللحم؟

Bring me this without meat please.
zhīblī hadī bla lham 'afak — جيب لي هد بلا اللحم عفاك

Does this contain egg?
wash fiha lbeiḍ? — واش فيها البيض؟

I'm allergic to ...
fīya whed hasasīya dyal ... — عندي الحساسية ديال . . .

I can't eat …	manqdersh nakūl ...	ما نقدرش نكول . . .
meat	lhem	اللحم
eggs	lbeiḍ	البيض
sugar	ssūkkar	سكر
chickpeas	Hums	حمص

EATING OUT

We would like a table for four please.
bghīna wahed ṭṭābla dyal rbeʿa 'afak — بغينا واحد الطباة ديال الربع عفاك

Please bring me the/a(n) ...	'afak zhīblī ...	عفاك جبلي . . .
menu	lmīnū	المينو
glass of water	wahed lkas dyal lma	واحد الكاس ديال الماء
ash tray	teffaya	طفاية
bill	lhsab	الحساب

bread	khebz	خبز
fork	lfershetta	لفيرشطة
knife	lmūs	لموس
spoon	lʿashek	لعاشق
napkin	lkālʿ	القلع
plate	tabstel	طبستل
pepper	lebrwa	لبراو
salt	melʜa	ملحة

Do you have ...?
wash ʿendkem ...? واش عندكم . . . ؟
Is service included in the bill?
wash sserbīs dakhel felhsab? واش سربيس داخل ف الحساب؟

What do you recommend?
Ash ghā tekhtār lī? اش غا تخطار لي؟
What are they eating?
Ash kayaklū? اش كيكلو؟
I would like what those people are eating.
bghīt hadakeshi lkyaklū hadūk lnās بغيت هدكشي لكيكلو هدوك الناس

What's in this?
Ash kein f hada? اش كاين ف هد؟
This is delicious.
hada bnīn هدا بنين
This isn't cooked well enough.
hadī maṭeibash mezyan هد ما طيباش مزيان

Utensils

cup/glass	kas	كاس
fork	fershetta	فرشيطة
knife	mūs	موس
plate	ṭebṣeil	طبيسل
spoon	mʿelqa	معلقة

FOOD

Useful Words

boiled	mslūq	مسلوق
bottle	qerʿa	قرعة
clean	nqī	نقي
cold	bared	بارد
delicious	bnīn	بنين
dirty	mwessekh	موسخ
empty	khawī	خاوي
fresh	trei	طري
fried	meqlī	مقلي
full	ʿamer	عامر
hot	skhūn	سخون
hot (spicy)	harr	حار
rare	maṭeiybsh bezzef	خضر
raw	ghḍer	غدر
ripe	tayeb	طايب
roasted	meshwī	مشوي
rotten	ghamezh	خامج
sour/unseasoned	mssūs	مسوس
stale	qdīm	قديم
sweet	hlew	حلو
warm	dafi	دافي
well done	teiyeb mezyan	طايب مزيان

STREET FOOD

An amazing variety of prepared food is offered by street vendors and in small stalls and shops throughout Morocco. Typically you'll find them wherever crowds gather, for example Djemaa-el-Fna in Marrakesh, or near train and bus stops.

What's that?
shnū hadak? شنو هدك؟
What's in it?
ash kein fiha f ldakhel? اش كاين فيها ف الداخل؟
What's he eating?
ash keiyakūl? اش كياكل؟
Please give me what he's eating.
ʿaṭeinī dakshī lī kayakūl hadak عطيني هد كشي لي كياكول هدك
Please give me a taste.
ʿaṭeinī wahed ḍūka 'afak عطيني ندوق عفاك
Please give me a little bit.
ʿaṭeinī wahed shwīya 'afak عطيني واحد شوي عفاك
We'd like to try that.
bghīna nzherrebū hadik بغينا نجربو هدك

... broshettes	qeṭban dyal ...	القطبان ديال ...
beef	bgrī	بكري
lamb	ghenemī	غنمي
liver	kebda	كبدة
heart	qelb	قلب
ground beef	kefta	كفتة

fava (broad) beans	lfūl	الفول
fried potatoes (chips)	frīt	بطاطا مقلية
peanuts	kawku	كاوكو
popcorn	lkelia	الكليا
rotisserie chicken	pūlī rūṭei	دجاج مشوي
salad	shalada	شلاضة
sandwich	kaskrūt	كسكروط
soup	ṣuba	صوبة

... eggs	beiḍ ...	بيض ...
scrambled	mterrba	مطربة
hard boiled	mslūqa	مصلوقة
fried	mqlīya	مقلية

FOOD

TYPICAL DISHES

Moroccan cuisine is delicious, visually striking, and varied. Here are some highlights of the country's rich culinary tradition:

ṭāzhīn

A thick and richly spiced stew named for the round dish with a cone-shaped cover in which it's prepared. Traditionally lamb or mutton, ṭāzhīn can also be made of beef, fish or poultry. Some of the most popular are lamb with prunes and onions, chicken with lemon, chicken with almonds and hard boiled eggs, and meatballs with eggs. The best are cooked over a charcoal brazier. In homes, ṭāzhīn is eaten from the dish in which it's cooked, placed in the centre of a low round table and eaten by hand with bread.

kūskūs/seksū

The most popular meal in North Africa, kūskūs consists of steamed semolina grain covered with a savoury meat and vegetable sauce. Kūskūs actually refers to the semolina grain, initially rolled by hand but now available dried and packaged. Again, an almost infinite number of variations are available. Two of the best are lamb with vegetables – most often including carrots, turnips, cabbage, pumpkin and squash – and lamb with raisins and onions. Customarily kūskūs is eaten by rolling it into a ball and popping it in your mouth. This is really an art and much more difficult than it looks – you might want to give it a try, but keep a spoon handy!

besṭeila

This is the well-known Moroccan delicacy made of chicken or pigeon, eggs, almonds, sugar and saffron, stuffed between many layers of a crisp, paper-thin pastry. A must when visiting the country, besṭeila can be specially ordered from many neighbourhood bakeries as well as the best Moroccan restaurants.

meshwī

Often found at weddings and other important occasions, meshwī is a complete lamb roasted and served in the centre of a table. Guests pull pieces of meat off with their hands and eat it with bread.

harīra

A thick, filling soup of tomatoes, lentils, chickpeas and meat seasoned with coriander and lemon. Traditionally used to break the fast during Ramadan, the Muslim month of fasting, harīra is now available at most Moroccan restaurants all year round.

atei benna'na

Mint tea in Morocco is not only a drink but a national institution, enjoyed in settings from Berber tents in the High Atlas to the King's Palace. Made with mint, green tea and sugar, each step in the preparation process appears carefully calculated, having been refined by countless repetitions. Expect many opportunities to experience the tea ritual first hand while staying in the country.

SELF-CATERING

When purchasing food for a quick meal, the most convenient place to go is the neighbourhood grocery shop – hanūt. You'll be amazed at the variety of different items contained in such a small area. Typically, almost everything you'll want is behind the counter so here's a good chance to practise your Arabic. Don't expect an orderly queue during busy times – you might need to be assertive to get any service.

Where's a nearby grocer's shop?
fīn kein shī hanūt dyal mwād lgheza'ya qrīb? — فين كاين شي حانوت ديال المواد الغذاءية قريب؟

How much is that?
beshhal hadīk? — بشحال هدك؟

Please give me a (half) kilo of cheese.
ʿaṭeinī wahed (neṣṣ) kīlū dyal frumazh — عطيني واحد (نص) كيلو الفورماجديال

Is there anything cheaper than that?
wash kein shī hazha rekheiṣa ʿala hadīk? — واش كاينة شي حاجة رخيصة علي هدك؟

Please give me a little bit of that.
ʿaṭeinī wahed shwīya min hadīk — عطيني واحد شوي من هدك

Add a little bit.
zīd shī shwīya — زيد شي شوي

Remove a little bit.
nqeṣ shī shwīya — نقص شي شوي

How much for ...?
bshhal ...? — بشحال ...؟

I don't want that one.
mabghītsh hadīk — مابغيت هدك

Please give me that other one.
'afak ʿteinī hadīk lakhūra — عفاك عطيني هدك لخري

Please give me ...	ʿaṭeinī shī ... ʿafak	عطيني شي ... عفاك
barley	shʿeir	شعير
bottled water	qerʿa dyal lma	قرعة ديال الماء
biscuits/sweets	helwat	حلوي

AT THE MARKET

Meat

beef	begrī	بكري
beef (ground)	kefta	كفتة
chicken	dzhazh	دجاج
heart	qelb	قلب
lamb	ghenmī	غنمي
liver	kebda	كبدة
meat	lhem	اللحم
pork	hellūf	حلوف
sausage	sūsīs	صوسسيص

FOOD

Seafood

anchovy	shṭun	شطون
cod	lamūrī	لاموري
eel	ṣemṭa	صمطة
lobster	lāngus	لانكوس
mussel	mūl	مول
sardine	serdīn	سردين
sea carp	qerb	قرب
shrimp	qeimrūn	قمرون
sole	ṣul	صول
squid	calamar	كالامار
tuna	ṭun	طون
whiting	merla	مرلة

Vegetables

artichoke	qūq	قوق
beans (green)	lūbīya	الوبية
cabbage	krum	كروم
capsicum/pepper		
(green)	felfla	فلفلة
(red)	felfla hemra	فلفلة حمرة
carrot	khīzū	خيزو
cauliflower	shīflūr	شيفلور
celery	krafes	كرافس
coriander	qeṣbur	كزبور
cucumber	khyar	خيار

eggplant	denzhal	دنجال
garlic	tūma	تومة
lettuce	kheṣṣ	خص
mushroom	feggīᶜ	فكيع
olive	zītūn	زيتون
onion	beṣla	بصلة
parsley	mᶜednūs	معدنوس
peas	zhelbana	جلبانة
potato	bṭāṭā	بطاطة
pumpkin/squash	gerᶜa hemra	كرعة حمرة
radish	fzhel	فجل
tomato	maṭeisha	مطيشة
turnip	left	لفت
vegetables	khuḍra	خضرة

Fruit

apple	teffah	تفاح
apricot	meshmash	مشماش
banana	bānān	بنان
cherries	hebb lemlūk	حب الملوك
date	tmer	تمر
fig	kermūs	كرموس
fruit	fakīya	فاكية
grapes	ᶜneb	عنب
lemon	hamed	حامض
orange	līmūn	ليمون
peach	khūkh	خوخ
pear	būᶜwīd	بوغويد
plum	berquq	برقوق
pomegranate	remman	رمان
prickly pear	kermūs lhendīya	كرموس الهندية
raisins	zbīb	زبيب
strawberries	tūt	توت
watermelon	dellah	دلاح

Dairy Products

butter	zebda	زبدة
buttermilk	lbcn	لبن
cheese	frumazh	فرماج
ice cream	laglas	لكلاس
milk	hlīb	حليب
yoghurt	danūn	دانون

Spices & Condiments

cinnamon	qerfa	قرفة
clove	qrunfel	قرونفل
cumin	kamūn	كمون
ginger	sken zhbīr	سكن جبير
hot pepper	felfla harra	فلفلة حارة
hot sauce	hrūr	حرور
jam	kunfitūr	كونفيتير
mustard	mūtard	موتارد
oil	zīt	زيت
olive oil	zīt lʿūd	زيت العود
paprika	felfla hamra	فلفلة حمرة
pepper	lebzār	البزار
salt	melha	ملحة
sugar	sūkkar	سكر
saffron	zaʿfran	زعفران
sesame	zhenzhlan	جنجلان

DRINKS

beer	bīra	بيرة
black tea	atei nnegru	اتاي نكرو
cold water	lma berd	الماء بارد
hot water	lma skhūn	الماء سخن
juice	ʿāṣeir	عصير
milk	hlīb	حليب
mint tea	atei bennaʿnaʿ	اتاي بنعنع
soft drink	munāḍa	مونادة
wine	shrab	شراب
coffee ...	qehwa ...	قهوة . . .
black	kehla	كحلة
with milk	belhlīb	بالحليب
with a little bit of milk	mherresa	محرسة

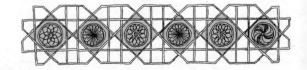

CAMPING

Where's the campsite?
  fīn kein lmukheyyem? فين كاين المخيم؟

Is there a site available?
  wash keina shī blāṣā khawīya? واش كاينة شي بلاصة خاوية؟

Is it OK for us to camp here?
  wesh makein mūshkīl īla kheyyemna henna? واش ما كين مشكل الي خيمنا هنا؟

Is there a shower?
  wash kein shī ḍūzh? واش كاين شي دوش؟

Where can I hire a tent?
  fīn yemkenlī nkrī shīgīṭūn? فين يمكن لي نكري شي كطون؟

backpack	ṣakkaḍō	صاك اضو
firewood	hteb	حطب
gas cartridge	bōṭa dyal lgaz	بوطة ديال الكاز
hammer	mterqa	مترقة
knife	mūs	لموس
rope	qenba	قنبة
sleeping bag	ṣak dyal kūsazh	صاك د كوساج
stove	furnu	فورنو
tent	gīṭūn	كيطون
torch/flash light	pīl	بيل

HIKING

Where can I find information about hiking in the area?

fīn yemken lī nelga shī mʿalūmat bash nḍōrū f had nahīya?

فين يمكن لي لقي شي معلومات باشنضورو ف هل النحية؟

I want to talk with someone who knows this area.

bghīt ntkellem mʿa shī wahed llī keiʿarf had nahīya

بغيت نتكلم مع شي واحد لي تيعرف هد الناحية

Where can I find a guide?

fīn yemkenlī nelga shī gīd? — فين يمكن لي نلقي شي كيد؟

How long is the hike?

shhal dyal lweqt kein f had ḍḍōra? — شحال ديال الوقت كاين ف هد ضورة؟

Is the trail well marked?

wash lʿalama beina? — واش العلامة باينة؟

Which is the shortest route?

'ashmen ṭrīq qrība? — اش من طريق قريبة؟

Is the trail open all year?

wash ṭrīq mehūla lʿam kūlū? — واش طريق محلولة العام كولو؟

Is the trail scenic?

wash trīq fīha shī menḍer? — واش طريق فيها شي مناظر؟

Where can I buy supplies?

fīn yemkenlī neshrī ʿwīn? — فين يمكن لي نشري العوين؟

On the path

Where have you come from?

mnīn zhītī? — منين جيتي؟

How long did it take you?

shhal dyal weqt keikheṣṣek? — شحال ديال الوقت كيخصك؟

Does this path go to ...?

wash had ṭrīq ghadīya l ...? — واش هد طريق غادية ل ...؟

altitude	ᶜlu	العلو
binoculars	shwafat	شوفات
cliff	ṣkher	صخر
climb (v)	ṭleᶜ	طلع
compass	bawṣala	بوصلة
downhill	habeṭ	هابط
forest	ghaba	غابة
guide	gīd	كيد
hike (n)	ḍōwira	ضورة
itinerary	ṭrīq	طريق
ledge	hashīya	الحاشية
map	kharīṭa	خريطة
mountain	zhbel	جبل
pass	triyqa	طريقة
peak	raṣ	راس
steep	qaseh	قاصح
uphill	ṭaleᶜ	طالع
valley	sehl	سهل
view	menḍer	منظر
village	duwwar	دوار
walk (v)	temsha ᶜla rezhlīn	تمش علا الرجلين

I'm lost.
tweḍḍert — تضرت

Where can we spend the night?
fīn yemken līna nbatū had līla? — فين يمكن لنا نباتو هد الليلة؟

Can I leave some things here?
wash neqder nkhellī shī hawezh hna? — واش نقدر نخلي شي حاجة هنا؟

AT THE BEACH

Is there a beach near here?
wash kein shī sheṭṭ qrīb l hna? واش كاين شي شاط قريب لهنا؟

Can we swim here?
wash nqedrū nʿūmū hna? واش نقدرو نعومو هنا؟

Is it safe to swim?
wash mashi khaṭar l ʿuman? واش ماشي خطر العومان؟

coast	muhīt	محيط
fishing	sīyada	صيادة
rock	hzher	حجر
sand	remla	رملة
sea	bher	بحر
sunblock	krīm dyal shems	كريم ديال الشمس
sunglasses	nḍaḍer dyal shems	الشمس نضاضر ديال
surfing	sōrf	سورف
swimming	ʿūman	العومان
towel	fōṭa	فوطة
waves	muzhat	موجات

WEATHER

How's the weather there?
kee dayer lzhū dyal temma? كي داير لجو ديال تما؟

Is it ... there?	wash kein ... temma?	واش كاين تما ...؟
hot	ṣṣehd	صهد
cold	lberd	البرد
cloudy	ḍḍbāba	ضباب

humid	rruṭuba	الرطوبة
raining	shṭa	الشتاء
snowing	ttelzh	الثلج
windy	rrīh	الريح

What's the temperature today?
shhal feddārāzhat dyal harara lyūm?
شحال فدراجات ديال الحرارة اليوم؟

What's the weather going to be like today?
kīfash ghādī ikūn lzhūw lyūm?
كفاش غادي يكون الجو اليوم؟

drought	zhafaf	الجفاف
dry	nashef	ناشف
flood	fayaḍan	الفيضان
lightning	breq	البرق
mud	ghīs	الغيس
rain	shta	الشتاء
rainbow	qẇas quzah	قوس قز
shade	ḍḍel	ضل
sky	sma	سماء
storm	ʿaṣifa	عاصفة
sun	shems	شمس
thunder	rʿad	رعد
weather	zhū	جو
wind	rīh	ريح

SEASONS

winter	shtwa	شتوا
spring	rbīᶜ	ربيع
summer	ṣeif	صيف
autumn/fall	khrīf	خريف

GEOGRAPHICAL TERMS

beach	laplāzh	شاطيء
bridge	qenṭra	قنطرة
cave	lakab	لكاب
cliff	skher	صخر
countryside	badīya	بادية
desert	ṣehra	صحراء
earthquake	zelzal	زلزال
farm	fīrma	فيرمة
forest	ghaba	غابة
harbor	mersa	مرسي
hill	haḍaba	هضبة
island	zhazīra	جزيرة
lake	ḍaya	ضاية
moon	qamar	قمر
mountain	zhbel	جبل
ocean	bhar	بحر
river	wad	واد

road	ṭraiq	طريق
rock	hezhra	حجرة
sand	remla	رملة
sun	shems	شمس
star	nzhma	نجمة
valley	wad	واد
waterfall	shellalat	شلالات

ANIMALS & INSECTS

bee	nehla	نحلة
bird	ṭeir	طير
butterfly	fertaṭō	فرطاطو
camel	zhmel	جمل
cat	meshsh	مش
chicken	dzhazha	دجاجة
cockroach	ṣerraq zzīt	سراق زيت
cow	begra	بكرة
deer	kurkdan	كركدان
dog	kelb	كلب
donkey	hmar	حمار
fish	hūta	حوتة
fly	debbana	دبانة
goat	meᶜza	معزة
horse	ᶜawd	العاود
monkey	qerd	قرد
mosquito	sniwala	سنيولة
mule	beghl	بغل
pig	hellūf	حلوف
rabbit	qnīya	قنية
rooster	ferrūzh	فروج
sheep	hawlī	حاولي
snail	babbūsh	بابوش
snake	hensh	حنش

spider	rtīla	رتيلة
squirrel	sebseb	سبسب
wild animal	Hayawan	حيوان

FLORA & AGRICULTURE

agriculture	felaha	فلاحة
bush	ghaba	غابة
crops	ṣaba	صبة
flower	werda	وردة
forest	ghaba	غابة
field	feddan	فدان
grass	rbī^{c}	ربيع
harvest (v)	hṣed	حصد
irrigation	sqa	سقا
leaf	werqa	ورقة
olive tree	shezhra dyal zzītūn	الزيتون شجرة ديال
plant	nebet	نبت
rose	werda	وردة
tree	shezhra	شجرة

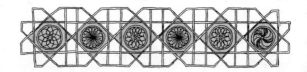

HEALTH

Anyone unfortunate enough to become ill will have no trouble finding the medicine they need at any chemist in a major city. Those who need a doctor have the choice of nationally funded health services or private doctors and clinics. You'll find the French language invaluable when dealing with the Moroccan medical system, as all doctors are educated in French and use it to write prescriptions and instructions for taking medicine.

Where's a/the ...?	fīn kein ...?	فين كاين . . . ؟
doctor	shī ṭbīb	شي طبيب
hospital	ṣṣebīṭār	صبيطار
chemist	lfārmasyan	الفرماسيان
dentist	shī ṭbīb dyal ssnan	طبيب ديال سنان

I'm sick.
ana mrīḍ — انا مريض

My friend is sick.
sahbī mrīḍ — صاحبي مريض

I need a doctor whospeaks English.
bghīt shī ṭbīb llī keihder nneglīzīya — بغيت واحد طبيب اللي كيحضر انكليزية

Can the doctor come here?
wash ṭṭbīb īqder īzhī l hna? — واش اقدر طبيب اجي لهنا؟

Can the doctor come with me?
wash ṭṭbīb īqder īzhī m'aya? — واش طبيب يقدر اجي معي

AILMENTS

I have a headache.
keiḍerrnī rāṣī — كايضرني راسي

I have a cold.
ana mrewweh — انا مروح

THE DOCTOR MAY SAY ...

What happened?
weqa'? — اش وقع؟

Do you feel any pain?
wash kathess beluwzh'? — واش كتحس ب لوجع؟

Where does it hurt?
fīn keiderrek? — فين كيضرك؟

Do you have a temperature?
wash fīk skhana? — واش فيك سخانة؟

How long have you been like this?
shhal hadī ū 'nta hakka? — شحال هد انت حق؟

Is this the first time you've had this?
wash hadī 'uwwela merra llī 'andek hadshī? — واش هيد اول مرة عندك هد شي؟

Are you taking any medication?
wash katakhōd shī dwa? — واش كتاخذ شي دوي؟

Do you smoke?
wash katkmī? — واش كتكمي؟

Do you drink?
wash katshreb? — واش كتشرب؟

Are you allergic to anything?
wash 'andek lhasasīya dyal shī hazha? — واش عندك الحساسية ديال شي حاجة؟

Are you pregnant?
wash 'ntī hamla? — واش انتي حاملة؟

HEALTH

I have a fever.
fīya skhana — فيي سخانة

I have diarrhoea.
kershī zharīya — كرشي جارية

I feel nauseous.
kanhess mekhūm — كنحس مكهوم

I'm constipated.
fīya lqabeṭ — فيي القبط

I've been vomiting.
kanteqqīya — كنتقيا

I can't sleep.
manqdersh nnᶜes — ماقدرش نعس

I feel ...	kanhess ...	كنحس...
dizzy	dayekh	دايخ
shivery	tbūrīsha	تبوريشة
weak	merkhī	مرخي

I have (a/an) ...	ᶜendi	عندي ...
allergy	lhasasīya	الحساسية
anaemia	ḍuᶜf feddem	ضعف في الدم
asthma	digga	ديقة
blister	mnebbel	منبل
bites	qrīṣ	قريص
burn	mehrōq	محروق
cancer	kunṣīr	كنسير
cold	lberd	البرد
cough	khba	كحبة
cut	zherha	جرحة
diabetes	merḍ ṣōkkar	مرض السكر
epilepsy	lrīyah	لرياح
heart condition	merḍ lqelb	مرض القلب
high blood pressure	laṭṭensīyu	لطنسيون
influenza	menzla	منزلة

HEALTH

infection	zhra	الجرحة
itch	hekka	الحكة
lice	gmel	الكمل
migrain	shqīqa	شقيقة
pain	lyzheᶜ	لوجع
rash	hbūb	حبوب
sore throat	hlaqem	حلاقم
stomach ache	lūzheᶜ f lmᶜda	لوجع ف المعدة
sunburn	lhrīq dyal shshemsh	لحرق ديال الشمس
tooth ache	luzheᶜ dyal ssnan	لوجع ديال لسنان
travel sickness	merda dyal ssafar	مرضة ديال السفر
worms	ddud	دود

Useful Words & Phrases

It hurts here.
keiḍernī henna — كيوجعني هنا

I feel better/worse.
kanhess hsen/kfes — كنحس احسن / كفيس

This is my usual medicine.
hada hūwa ddwa dyal dīma — هد هو دوي ديالي ديما

I've been vaccinated.
dert zhelba — درت جلبة

I don't want a blood transfusion.
mabghīts ndīr ddemm — ما بغيتش ندير دم

Please give me the bill.
ᶜafak ᶜṭainī lhsab — عفاك عطيني الحساب

My ... hurts.	katḍerrnī ...	كتضرني . . .
back	ḍehrī	ضهري
hand	yeddī	يدي
leg/foot	rezhlī	رجلي
Is it broken?	wash mherresa?	واش مهرسة؟
Is it sprained?	wash mfdūʿ?	واش مفدوع؟
I'm bleeding.	kansīl beddem	كنسيل بدم
accident	ksīda	كسيدا
addiction	blīya	بلية
AIDS	sīda	سيدا
bandage	bunda	بندة
blood group	nuwʿ dyal ddem	النوع ديال الدم
blood pressure	laṭṭensīyu	لطانسيون
blood test	thlīl dyal ddem	تحليل ديال الدم
burn	herqa	حرقة
contagious	keitʿada	كيتعد
cream/ointment	pumada	بوماد
dangerous	khāṭār	خطر
infected	mʿeffen	معفن
injection	shūka	شوكة
laboratory	mukhtabar	مختبر
medicine	ddawa	دوي
nurse	fermlīya	فرملية
pain	hrīq/wzheʿ	حريق / وجع
patient	lmrīd.	المريض
poison	semm	سم
sanitary	ṣhhī	صحي
swell (v)	nfekh	نفخ
syringe	huqna	حقنة
test (laboratory)	thlīl	تحليل
urine	bōl	بول
vitamin	vītamīn	فيتامين

WOMEN'S HEALTH

Can I see a female doctor?
wash neqder nshūf shī ṭbība dyal lᶜyalet?
واش نقدر نشوف طبيبة ديال العيلات؟

I prefer a woman.
kanfḍel lmra
كنفضل امراة

I'm pregnant.
ana hamla
انا حاملة

I'd like to take a pregnancy test.
bghīt nuwwez thlīl dyal lhmel
بغيت ندوز تحليلات علي الحمل

I haven't had my period for ... weeks.
mahanīsh hak ... shahr ldām
محانيش . . . حق شهر الدم

contraception	ḍed lhmal	منع الحمل
diaphragm	dyafram	ديافراكم
menstruation	heq shher	حق الشهر

SPECIAL HEALTH NEEDS

I'm ...	ana ...	انا . . .
anaemic	faqer f ddemm	فقر ف الدم
asthmatic	fīya ddīga	في ديقة
diabetic	fīya merḍ ssukkar	في مرض السكر

I've got high/low blood pressure.
ᶜandī lattensìyu taleᶜ/nazel
عندي لطنسيون طالع / نازل

I have a weak heart.
ᶜandī lqelb dᶜīf
عندي القلب ضعيف

HEALTH

I take regular medication.
kandawem dwa — كنداوم دوي

I'm on a special diet.
kan dīr rrīzhīm — داير رجيم

I have my own syringe.
ʿandī shūka dyalī — عندي شوكة ديالي

I'm allergic to ...	ʿandī lhsasīya mʿa ...	عندي الحساسية مع . . .
bees	nhel	نحل
dairy products	makla llī fīha lhlīb	مكلة اللي فيها الحليب
penicillin	lbīnselīn	بنسلين
this	hadī	هد

PARTS OF THE BODY

arm	dreʿ	درع
back	ḍher	ضهر
blood	demm	دم
bone	ʿḍem	عضم
chest	ṣder	صدر
ear	wden	ودن
eye	ʿīn	عين
face	wzheh	وجه
finger	ṣbeʿ	صبع
foot	rzhel	رجل
hair	shʿar	شعار
hand	yedd	يد
head	rāṣ	راس
heart	qelb	قلب
leg	rzhel	رجل
liver	kebda	كبد
lung	reyya	رية
mouth	fūmm	فوم
shoulder	ktef	كتف

skin	zheld	جلد
teeth	snan	سنان
throat	hleq	الحلق
toe	ṣbeᶜ	صبع
tongue	lsan	لسنان

AT THE CHEMIST

Do you have medicine for (a) ...?	wash ᶜandek ddwa dyal ...?	واش عندك دوي ديال . . .؟
cold	rrewwah	رواح
cough	lkehha	الكحة
diarrhoea	sshal	سهال
headache	rraṣ	الراس
sore throat	lhlaqem	الحلقم
stomachache	wazheᶜ lmᶜda	وجع المعدة

Do I need a prescription?
wash kheṣṣnī shī werqa dyal ṭṭbīb?
واش خصني شي ورقة ديال الطبيب؟

How many should I take each time?
sHal men waHda ghadī nakūl kūl merra?
شحال من واحدة غادي ناكل كل مرة؟

How many times per day?
shhal men merra fennhar?
شحال من مرة ف النهار؟

antibiotics	'antībīyutīk	انتيبيوتيك
aspirin	asperīn	اسبرين
bandage	banda	باندا
condoms	kapūt	كبوط
contraceptives	dwa dyal lhmel	دوي ضد الحمل
gauze	faṣma	فاصمة
pain killers	muhdden	مهدن
sleeping pills	dwa dyal nnᶜas	دوي ديال النعس

AT THE DENTIST

I have a toothache.
fīya ddersa — في ضرسة

I've got a cavity.
fīya ssūsa — في صوسة

I've lost a filling.
taht līya lʿmara dyal ddersa — طاحت لي العمر ديال ضرسة

I've broken a tooth.
therresat līya ssenna — تهرست لي السنة

My gums hurt.
keyḍerrnī lhem dyal ssnan — كيضرني لحم ديال سنان

Don't extract it!
matgleʿhash! — ماتكلعهاش!

Give me an anaesthetic!
dīr līya lbenzh! — در لي البنج!

AT THE OPTOMETRIST

I want my eyes tested.
bhīt ndewwez ʿala ʿīnī — بغيت ندوز علي عيني

I'm long/short sighted.
makanshūfsh bʿaīd/qrīb — ما كنشوفش بعيد / قريب

Please fix my glasses.
ʿafak ṣoweb nndader dyalī — عفاك صوب لي نضاضر ديالي

I'd like new glasses.
bghīt ndader zhdad — بغيت نضاضر جداد

I'd like new contact lenses.
bghīt lʿadadsat dyal lʿinìn zhdad — بغيت عدسات ديال العنين جداد

I'd like contact lens solution.
bghīt lmadda llī keighslū bīha lʿadadsat dyal lʿinìn

بغيت المادة اللي كيغسلو بها العدسات للعنين

DISABLED TRAVELLERS

I'm ...	ana ...	انا . . .
disabled/handicapped	muʿewweq	معوق
blind	ʿma	عمي
deaf	smek	سمك

I need assistance.
bhīt llī īwqef mʿya — بغيت لي يوقف معي

Do you have services for disabled people?
wesh keina shī meslaha mekhtaṣṣa belmuʿewweqīn? — واش كاين شي مصلحة مختصة بالمعوقين؟

Is there wheelchair access?
wesh keina shī kerrusa dyal lmuʿewwaqīn? — واش كاين شي كروسة ديال االمعوقين؟

Speak louder please.
tkellem bezhzhhed ʿafak — تكلم ب جهد عفاك

Speak more slowly please.
tkellem beshwīya ʿafak — تكلم ب شوية عفاك

DID YOU KNOW ...

Moroccans can be very sensitive about of their Royal Family - the King claims direct descent from the Prophet, and criticism of him may be viewed as blasphemous.

Will there be a guide to explain things?
wesh kein shī murshed? واش كاين شي مرشد؟

I'm hard of hearing.
ʿandī ssmeʿ tqīl عندي سمع تقيل

I have a hearing aid.
ʿandī lapparay dyal ssmeʿ عندي لبراي ديال سمع

Are guide dogs permitted?
wesh lkelb llī kaygiyyid lʿma mesmuh līh īdkhel? واش الكلب يلي كيكيد العمي مسموح ليه ادخل؟

TRAVELLING WITH A FAMILY

I'm travelling with my family.
ana mṣafer mʿa lʿalla dyalī انا مسافر مع العايلة ديالي

Are there facilities for babies?
wesh kein tshīlat dyal ddrarī ṣghar? واش كاين تسهيلات ديال دراري صغار؟

Are there going to be other families?
wesh ghadī īkūnū lʿa'īlat akhrin? واش غادي يكونو العاءلات اخرين؟

Do you have a baby-sitting service?
wesh kein ʿandkum dar lhaḍana? واش كاين عندكم دار لحضانة؟

Where can I find an English-speaking baby-sitter?

fīn yemken llī nelga wahed lmurabbīya dyal ddrarī ṣṣghar llī keitkellem benneglīzīya?

فين يمكن لي نلقي واحد المربية ديال دراري صغار لي كيتكلم بانكليزية؟

Can you put an extra bed in the room?

wesh teqder ddīr wahed ssrīr dyal drarī ṣghar zayd felbīt?

واش تقدر تدير واحد سرير ديال دراري صغار زايد ف البيت؟

I need a car with a child seat.

bghīt wahed ṭṭōmōbīl belkōrsī dyal drarī ṣghar

بغيت واحد طوموبيل بالكرسي ديال دراري صغار

Is it suitable for children?

wesh mnaseb l drarī ṣghar?

واش مناسب لدراري صغار؟

Body Language

Public displays of affection are common between friends of the same sex, but frowned on between couples, even when married. Handshakes, kisses and hugs are all common greetings.

Are there any activities for children?
wesh kein shī tanshīṭ dyal drarī ṣghar?
واش كاين شي تنشيط ديال
دراري صغار؟

Is there a family discount?
wesh ken shī tekhfīṭ bennsiba lʿa'īla?
واش كاين شي تخفيض بالنسبة
للعائلة؟

Are children allowed?
wesh mesmuh l drarī?
واش مسموح للدراري؟

Is there a playground nearby?
wesh kein shī ssaha dyal llʿeb qrība?
كاين شي الساحة ديال اللعب
واش قريبة؟

TIMES, DATES & FESTIVALS

TELLING THE TIME

Telling the time in Morocco is fairly straightforward. The abbreviations 'am'and 'pm' are expressed in whole words, for example, '8 am' is literally '8 in the morning', ttmenya feṣṣbah; '2 pm' is '2 in the afternoon', zhzhūzh felᶜshīya; and '8 pm' is '8 at night', ttmenya fellīl

Hours

It's ... o'clock	hadī ...	هادي ...
1	lewhda	الوحدة
2	zhzhūzh	جوج
3	ttlata	تلاتة
4	rreb"a	اربعة
5	lkhamsa	خمسة
6	ssetta	ستة
7	sseb"a	سبعة
8	ttmenya	ثمنية
9	ttsᶜūd	تسعود
10	lᶜashra	عشرة
11	lhdash	حضاش
12	ṭṭnash	طناش

morning	feṣṣbah	صباح
afternoon	felᶜshīya	عشية
night	fellīl	ليلا

hour	saᶜa	ساعة
two hours	saᶜatein	ساعتين
more than two hours	swayeᶜ	سوية

What time is it?	shal fessaᶜa?	شحال فالساعة؟
It's three exactly.	hadī ttlata nīshan	هادي تلاتة نيشان
It's about four.	hadī rrebᶜa teqrīben	هادي ربعة تقريبا

Minutes

Minutes are expressed after the hour and divided into groups of five. The literal translation gives an idea of how the system works.

It's ...	hadī ...	هادي . . .
1.05 (one and one five minute period)	lewhda ūqṣem	الواحدة وقسم
1.10 (one and two five minute periods)	lewhda ūqeṣmein	الواحدة و قسمين
1.15 (one and 1/4)	lewhda ūrbâᶜ	الواحدة وربع
1.20 (one and 1/3)	lewhda ūtūlūt	الواحدة و تلت
1.25 (one and 25)	lewhda ūkhamsa ūᶜshrīn	الواحدة و خمسة و عشرين
1.30 (one and 1/2)	lewheda ūneṣṣ	الواحدة و نص
1.35 (two less 25)	zhzhūzh qell khamsa ūᶜshrīn	جوج قل خمسة و عشرين
1.40 (two less 1/3)	zhzhūzh qell tūlūt	جوج قل تلت
1.45 (two less 1/4)	zhzhūzh llarūb	جوج الا ربع
1.50 (two less two five minute periods)	zhzhūzh qell qeṣmein	جوج قل قسمين
1.55 (two less one five minute period)	zhzhūzh qell qṣem	جوج قل قسم

minute	dqīqa	دقيقة
minutes	dqayeq	دقايق
second	tanīya	تانية
seconds	tanīyat	تانيات
five minutes	qṣem	قسم
ten minutes	qeṣmein	قسمين

DAYS

Sunday	nhar lhedd	نهار الحد
Monday	nhar letnīn	نهار لتنين
Tuesday	nhar ttlat	نهار تلات
Wednesday	nhar larbᶜ	نهار لاربع
Thursday	nhar lekhmīs	نهار لخميس
Friday	nhar zhzhemᶜa	نهار جمع
Saturday	nhar ssebt	نهار سبت

What day is it today?	shnū lyūm?	شنو ليوم؟

day	nhar	نهار
two days	yūmein	يومين
three days	teltīyam	تلتيام
this week	had l'ūsbūᶜ/ssīmana	هداالاسبوع / سيمانا
two weeks	zhūzhdel'asabīᶜ/ dessīmanat	جوج دل اسابيع / دسيمانات

MONTHS

Morocco operates on two calendar systems – the standard Western, or Gregorian system, and the Muslim calendar. In general, all business and government affairs are conducted by the Western calendar and this is the one you'll need to know.

The Muslim calendar, used in Morocco mainly for religious holidays, consists of a 354 day year divided into 12 lunar months. A day is added to the last month 11 times in every 30 years, so that in a century the Muslim calendar differs from the Gregorian calendar by just over two years. The first day of the first year corresponds to 15 July 622 AD, the year in which Mohammed and his followers migrated from Mecca to Medina.

January	zhanvīyeh	جنفيه
February	fevrīyeh	ففريه
March	mars	مارس
April	abrīl	ابريل
May	mayyū	مايو
June	yūnyū	يونيو
July	yūlyūz	يوليوز
August	ghūsht	غشت
September	sebtamber	سبتمبر
October	'ūktūber	اكتوبر
November	nūvamber	نفمبر
December	dīsamber	دسمبر
a month	shher	شهر
two months	shehrein	شهرين
three months	telt shhūr	تلت شهور
a year	ʿam	عام
two years	ʿamein	عامين
three years	telt snīn	تلت سنين

PRESENT

now	daba	دابا
today	lyūm	ليوم
this month	had shshhar	هدا الشهر
this year	had lʿam	هدا العام

PAST

yesterday	lbareh	لبارح
day before yesterday	wellbareh	وللبارح
yesterday morning	lbareh feṣṣbah	لبارح ف لصباح
last week	l'ūsbūʿ llī fat	الاسبوع الي فات
last month	shshhar llī fat	الشهر الي فات
last year	lʿam llī fat	العام الي فات

FUTURE

an hour from now	men daba wahed ssaʿa	من دابا واحد الساعة
tomorrow	ghedda	غدا
tomorrow afternoon	ghedda felʿshīya	غدا ف العشية

Psst ...

People may try to get your attention by making a hissing sound. It's used by motorists as a warning to get out of the way, and also as the equivalent of a wolf whistle.

day after tomorrow	bᶜd ghedda	بعد غدا
next week	l'ūsbūᶜ llī zhei	الاسبوع الي جاي
a week from today	bhal lyūm	بحال ليوم
next month	shshhar llī zhei	الشهر الي جاي
next year	lᶜam llī zhei	العام الي جاي

around	zhwayeh	جوايح
on time	felweqt	فالوقت
early	bekrī	بكري
late	mᶜeṭṭel	معطل
hurry up	serbī	سربي
early in the morning	feṣṣbāh bekrī	ف صباح بكري
past	lmāḍei	لماضين
present	lhāḍer	لحاضر
future	lmūsteqbal	لمستقبل

FESTIVALS

Morocco has a number of religious and government holidays representing the country's rich historical and cultural traditions. Since the Muslim holidays are based on the Islamic calender, the date of their occurence will vary from year to year.

dessīmanatd?

Ramadan ramadan رمضان

This is the Islamic month of fasting. From sunrise to sunset each day, Muslims refrain from eating, drinking, smoking and other worldly pleasures unless they're ill, pregnant, nursing, travelling, below the age of puberty or otherwise unable. Obviously this causes major disruptions in the pattern of daily life. Businesses usually open mid-morning and close around 4 pm. During the day, activity slows down considerably only to increase in the evening as the cafes and streets remain full until after midnight. While Ramadan can present problems for travellers, in many ways it's an exciting time to be in the country. The religious significance combined with the festive atmosphere in the evenings and many special foods make it a favourite time of year for many Moroccans.

One word of advice during Ramadan, be sensitive to those who are fasting during the day. When possible try not to eat, drink or smoke in public and make an effort to dress conservatively.

fasting	ssīyam	الصيام
Are you fasting?	wash 'nta ṣeim?	واش انت صايم ؟
Where are you going to break the fast?	fīn ghadī tefṭer?	فين غادي تفطر؟

Aid el kbir ʿīd lkbīr عيد الكبير

Probably the most important religious holiday of the year, Aid el kbir is when Muslims celebrate Abraham's willingness to sacrifice his son. Most families buy a sheep to sacrifice after morning prayers and then eat throughout the day.

Throne day ʿīd lʿarsh عيد العرش

This, the most significant government holiday, celebrates King Hassan II's ascension to the throne. Festivities include parades and traditional concerts throughout the country.

Where's the parade?
fīn ghadī īkūn l'istiʿrad? — فين غادي يكون الاستعراض؟

When will the parade begin?
'imta ghadī ībda l'istiʿrad? — امتي غادي يبدآ الاستعراض؟

Will there be a concert today?
wash ghadi īkūn sh ṭṭarab lyum? — واش غادي يكون الطرب اليوم؟

NUMBERS & AMOUNTS

Due to its colonisation by France, Morocco uses standard Western numerical symbols rather than those normally associated with Arab countries.

CARDINAL NUMBERS

1	wahed	واحد
2	zhūzh	جوج
3	tlata	تلاتة
4	reb^{c}a	ربعة
5	khamsa	خمسة
6	setta	ستة
7	seb^{c}a	سبعة
8	tmenya	تمنية
9	tes^{c}ūd	تسعود
10	^{c}asḥra	عشرة

'uh-oh'

The glottal stop in Moroccan Arabic is also heard in English - it's the sound made between the vowels in 'uh-oh'

11	hḍāsh	حضاش
12	ṭnāsh	طناش
13	telṭāsh	تلطاش
14	rbaᶜṭāsh	ربعطاش
15	khamsṭāsh	خمسطاش
16	seṭṭāsh	سطاش
17	sbeᶜṭāsh	سبعطاش
18	tmenṭāsh	تمنطاش
19	tseᶜṭāsh	تسعطاش
20	ᶜashrīn	عشرين
21	wahed ūᶜashrīn	واحد و عشرين
22	tnein ūᶜashrīn	تنين و عشرين
23	tlata ūᶜashren	تلاتة و عشرين
30	tlatīn	تلاتين
40	rebᶜīn	ربعين
50	khamsīn	خمسين
60	settīn	ستين
70	sebᶜīn	سبعين
80	tmanīn	تمانين
90	tesᶜīn	تسعين
100	mya	مية
200	myatein	ميتين
300	teltmya	تلات مية
400	rbaᶜmya	ربع مية
500	khemsmya	خمس مية
600	settemya	ست مية
700	sbeᶜmya	سبع مية
800	temnemya	تمن مية
900	tseᶜmya	تسع مية
1000	alf	الف
2000	alfein	الفين
3000	telt alaf	تلت الاف
10,000	ᶜashra alaf	عشرة الاف
100,000	meyat alf	مية الف

one million	melyūn	مليون
two million	zhūzh delmlein	جوج د الملايين
one billion	melyar	مليار

Multiples

To form multiples, simply string the appropriate numbers together, separating them with ū.

225	myatein ūkhamsa ūᶜshrīn	ميتين و خمسة و عشرين
1989	alf ūtseᶜmeyya	الف و تسع مية و
	ūtsᶜūd ūtmanīn	تسعود و ثمانين

ORDINAL NUMBERS

first	lūwwel	الاول
second	tanī	تاني
third	talet	تالت
fourth	rabeᶜ	رابع
fifth	khames	خامس
sixth	sades	سادس
seventh	sabeᶜ	سابع
eighth	tamen	تامن
ninth	taseᶜ	تاسع
tenth	ᶜasher	عاشر

the first bus	lkar llūwwel	الكار الاول
the third street	zzenqa ttalta	الزنقة تالتة

to count	hseb	حسب
equal	bhal bhal	بحال بحال
half	neṣṣ	نص
a quarter	rbe^c	ربع
per cent	felmya	فلمية

BERBER

The Berber language is spoken throughout North Africa, with speakers concentrated in Morocco and Algeria. An ancient people with a reputation as fierce warriors, the Berbers have notoriously resisted outside control, managing to maintain their language and cultural practices under Roman, Vandal and Arab rule. Today the Berber people of Morocco largely inhabit mountain regions and parts of the desert. There are three main ethnic groups, which can be loosely identified by dialect.

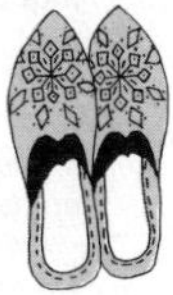

In the north, centred on the Rif, the locals speak a dialect which has been called Riffian and is spoken as far south as Figuig on the Algerian frontier. The dialect that predominates in the Middle and High Atlas and the valleys leading into the Sahara goes by various names, including Braber or Amazigh.

More settled tribes of the High Atlas, Anti-Atlas, Souss Valley and south-western oases generally speak Tashelhit or Chleuh. The following phrases are a selection from the Tashelhit dialect, the one visitors are likely to find most useful.

Berber may be written in Arabic or Roman script, although the Berbers have traditionally maintained an oral culture transmitted from generation to generation through storytelling and song.

You Should Know

Is there ...?	ees eela ...?
Do you have ...?	ees daroon ...?
I want ...	reeh ...
Give me ...	feeyee ...
How much is it?	minshk aysker?
food	teeremt
water	amen
mule	aserdon
somewhere to sleep	kra lblast mahengwen
big/small	mqorn/eemzee
a lot/little	bzef/eemeek
too expensive	nuqs emeek
no good	oor eefulkeemqorn/ eemzee
today	zig sbah
tomorrow	ghasad
yesterday	eegdam

MEETING PEOPLE

Hello.	la bes darik/darim (m/f)
Hello (in response).	la bes
Goodbye.	akayaoon arbee
Please.	barakalaufik
Thank you.	barakalaufik
Yes.	eyeh
No.	oho

Excuse me.	semhee
How are you?	meneek antgeet?
Fine, thank you.	la bes, lhamdulah
Good.	eefulkee/eeshwa
Bad.	khaib
See you later.	akrawes dah inshallah

GETTING AROUND

I want to go to ...	reeh ...
Where is (the) ...?	mani heela ...?
mountain	adrar
pass	tizee
river	aseet
village	doorwar
Is it far/close?	ees yagoog/eeqareb?
straight	neeshan
to the right	fofaseenik
to the left	fozelmad

NUMBERS

1	yen	6	sddes
2	seen	7	sa
3	krad	8	tem
4	koz	9	tza
5	smoos	10	mrawet

11	yen d mrawet
12	seen d mrawet
20	ashreent
21	ashreent d yen d mrawet
22	ashreent d seen d mrawet
30	ashreent d mrawet
40	snet id ashreent
50	snet id ashreent d mrawet
100	smoost id ashreent/meeya

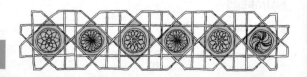

FRENCH

The most commonly spoken European language in Morocco is French, a legacy of Morocco's time as a French protectorate from 1912 until independence was regained in 1956. If the thought of getting your tongue around Arabic is too much, it would be a good investment to learn some French.

The following words and phrases should help you communicate in French on a basic level:

PRONUNCIATION

French pronunciation can be difficult for an English speaker but if you remember a few basic rules, you won't have any trouble making yourself understood.

Vowels

a	as in the 'u' in 'cup'
e	barely pronounced, as the 'e' in 'open'
é	as the 'ay' in 'may'
è	as the 'e' in 'merry', but slightly longer
i	as in 'hit'
o	as in British 'pot'
u	to make this sound, purse you lips as if you were saying 'oo' but make the sound 'ee'

Diphthongs (Vowel Combinations)

ai	as the 'e' in 'bet' but a bit longer
eu	as the 'er' in British 'berth' but shorter
oi	sounds like 'wa'
ui	sounds like 'wi'
au	as the 'o' in 'or'
eau	as the 'ow' in 'show'
ou	as the 'oo' in 'book'

Consonants

These are generally pronounced as they are in English but there are some you should note. Consonants appearing at the end of a word aren't pronounced, unless they run on to a following word.

c	hard, like 'k' before a, o and u soft, like 's', before e, i and y
ç	always soft, like 's'
g	hard, as in 'get', before a, o and u soft, as in 'germ', before e and i
h	silent
j	as the 's' in measure
q	as 'k'
s	between two vowels, it's pronounced as 'z' elsewhere, as the 's' in 'sit'
l	always pronounced with the tip of the tongue touching the back of the upper incisors, and the surface of the tongue higher than for an English 'l'. Be especially careful to maintain this tongue position for 'l's at the ends of words, as in il
r	produced by moving the bulk of the tongue backwards to constrict the air flow in the pharynx, while the tip of the tongue rests behind the lower front teeth. It's quite similar to the noise made by some people before spitting, but with much less friction.

Subject Pronouns

I	je
you	tu (sg & inf)
he/it	il
she/it	elle
we	nous
you	vous (pl & pol)
they	ils/elles (m/f)

Question Words

Why?	Pourquoi?
Which?	Quel?
When?	Quand?
Where?	Où?
Who?	Qui?

MEETING PEOPLE

Greetings & Civilities

Hello./Good morning.	Bonjour.
Goodbye.	Au revoir/Salut.
Good evening.	Bonsoir.
(Have a) good evening.	Bonne soirée.
Good night.	Bonne nuit.
Please.	S'il vous plaît.
Thank you.	Merci.
You're welcome.	De rien/Je vous en prie.
Yes.	Oui.
No.	Non.
No, thank you.	Non, merci.
Excuse me.	Excusez-moi/Pardon.
How are you?	Comment allez-vous/Ça va?
Well, thanks.	Bien, merci.
big/small	grand/petit
open/closed	ouvert/fermé

Making Conversation

What's your name?	Comment vous/appelez-vous?
My name is ...	Je m'appelle ...
How old are you?	Quel âge avez-vous?
I'm 25.	J'ai vingt-cinq ans.

Where are you from?	D'où êtes-vous?
I'm/We're from ...	Je viens/Nous venons ...
America	de l'Amérique
Australia	de l'Australie
Canada	du Canada
England	de l'Angleterre
Germany	de l'Allemagne
Italy	de l'Italie
Japan	du Japon
The Netherlands	des Pays Bas
Spain	de l'Espagne
Sweden	du Suède
Switzerland	de la Suisse

Language Difficulties

Do you speak English?	Parlez-vous anglais?
I understand.	Je comprends.
I don't understand.	Je ne comprends pas.

GETTING AROUND

I want to go to ...	Je veux aller à ...
What is the fare to ...?	Combien coûte le billet pour ...?
How far is ...?	À combien de kilomètres est ...?

When does the ... leave/arrive?	À quelle heure part/arrive ...?
bus	l'autobus
intercity bus/coach	le car
train	le train
boat	le bateau
ferry	le bac
Where's the ...?	Où est ...?
bus station for ...	la gare routière pour ...
train station	la gare
ticket office	la billeterie/le guichet
street	la rue
city	la ville
village	le village
bus stop	l'arrêt d'autobus
Which bus goes to ...?	Quel autobus/car part pour ...?
Does this bus go to ...?	Ce car-là va-t-il à ...?
How many buses per day go to ...?	Il y a combien de cars chaque jour pour ...?
Please tell me when we arrive in ...	Dîtes-moi s'il vous plaît à quelle heure on arrive ...
Stop here, please.	Arrêtez ici, s'il vous plaît.
Please wait for me.	Attendez-moi ici, s'il vous plaît.
May I sit here?	Puis-je m'asseoir ici?
Where can I rent a bicycle?	Où est-ce que je peux louer une bicyclette?
address	adresse
air-conditioning	climatisation
airport	aéroport
camel	chameau
car	voiture
crowded	beaucoup de monde

daily	chaque jour
donkey	âne
horse	cheval
number	numéro
ticket	billet
Wait!	Attendez!

Directions

left/right	gauche/droite
here/there	ici/là
next to	à côté de
opposite	en face
behind	derrière
north	nord
south	sud
east	est
west	ouestici/là

ACCOMMODATION

Where is the hotel?	Où est l'hôtel?
Can I see the room?	Peux-je voir la chambre?
How much is this room per night?	Combien est cette chambre pour une nuit?
Do you have any cheaper rooms?	Avez-vous des chambres moins chères?
That's too expensive.	C'est trop cher.
This is fine.	A va bien.
bed	lit
blanket	couverture
camp site	camping
full	complet
hot water	eau chaude

key	clef/clé
roof	terrasse
room	chambre
sheet	drap
shower	douche
toilet	les toilettes
washbasin	lavabo
youth hostel	auberge de jeunesse

AROUND TOWN

Where is the ...?	Où est ...?
bank	la banque
barber	le coiffeur
beach	la plage
embassy	l'ambassade
market	le marché
mosque	la mosqueé
museum	le museé
old city	le centre historique
palace	le palais
pharmacy	la pharmacie
police station	la police
post office	la poste
restaurant	le restaurant
university	l'université
zoo	le zoo

I want to change ...	Je voudrais changer ...
money	de l'argent
US$	des dollars américains
UK	des livres sterling
A$	des dollars australie
DM	des marks allemands
travellers cheques	des chèques de voyage

INTERESTS

I like ...	J'aime bien ...
caving	la spéléologie
cooking	la cuisine
dancing	la danse
painting	un tableau
singing	le chant
travelling	les voyages

What sort of music do you like?
Quel genre de musique aimes-tu?

What do you think of ...? Qu'est-ce que vous pensez de ...?

I think it's ...	Je pense que c'est ...
boring	ennuyeux
exciting	genial/super
expensive	cher

Drugs

If you find yourself in a situation where drugs are being discussed, the following phrases might help you understand the conversation, but if referring to your own interests, use discretion.

Do you smoke?	Tu fumes?
I'm stoned	Je suis cassé/e.
I'm not interested	Ca ne m'intéresse pas.
I don't take drugs	Je ne prends pas de drogue.

I take ... occasionally	Je prends du (m)/de la (f) ... occasionnellement.
marijuana	à la marijuana
hash	au haschich
heroin	à l'héroïne
cocaine	à la cocaïne
amphetamines	aux amphétamines
acid	à l'acide
drugs	aux drogues

SHOPPING

Where can I buy ...?	Où est-ce que je peux acheter ...?
How much?	Combien?
How much does it cost?	Ça coûte combien?
more/less	plus/moins
too much	trop cher
Do you have (a) ...?	Avez-vous ...?
stamps	des timbres
newspaper	un journal
batteries	des piles
matches	des allumettes
milk	du lait
matches	des allumettes
mineral water	de l'eau minérale

HEALTH

I'm sick.	Je suis malade.
I feel weak.	Je me sens faible.
It hurts here.	J'ai une douleur ici.
I feel nauseous.	J'ai des nausèes.
I have ...	J'ai ...
an allergy	une allergie
diarrhoea	la diarrhèe
influenza	la grippe
a stomachache	mal au ventre
a veneral disease	une maladie venerienne

TIME, DATES & NUMBERS

Time

today	aujourd'hui
tomorrow	demain
yesterday	hier
now	maintenant
morning	matin
afternoon	après-midi
evening	soir
day/night	jour/nuit
week/month/year	semaine/mois/an
What's the time?	Quelle heure est-il?
At what time?	À quelle heure?
after	après
on time	à l'heure
early	tôt
late	tard
quickly	vite
slowly	lentement

Days

Monday	lundi
Tuesday	mardi
Wednesday	mercredi
Thursday	jeudi
Friday	vendredi
Saturday	samedi
Sunday	dimanche

Months

January	janvier
February	février
March	mars
April	avril
May	mai
June	juin
July	juillet
August	août
September	septembre
October	octobre
November	novembre
December	décembre

Cardinal Numbers

0	zéro	10	dix
1	un	11	onze
2	deux	12	douze
3	trois	13	treize
4	quatre	14	quatorze
5	cinq	15	quinze
6	six	16	seize
7	sept	17	dix-sept
8	huit	18	dix-huit
9	neuf	19	dix-neuf

20	vingt	100	cent
21	vingt-et-un	101	cent un
22	vingt-deux	125	cent vingt-cinq
30	trente	200	deux cents
40	quarante	300	trois cents
50	cinquante	400	quatre cents
60	soixante	1000	mille
70	soixante-dix	2000	deux milles
80	quatre-vingts	3000	trois milles
90	quatre-vingt-dix	4000	quatre milles

Ordinal Numbers

first	premier	eighth	huitième
second	deuxième	ninth	neufième
third	troisième	tenth	dixième
fourth	quatrième	twentieth	vingtième
fifth	cinquième	thirtieth	trentième
sixth	sixième	fortieth	quarantième
seventh	septième	fiftieth	cinquantième

EMERGENCIES

Call a doctor!	Appelez un médecin!
Call the police!	Appelez la police!
Help me please!	Au secours/Aidez-moi!
Thief!	(Au) voleur!

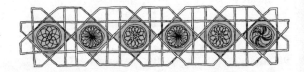

EMERGENCIES

Help!	ᶜṭeqnī!	عتقني!
Stop!	wqef!	وقف!
Go away!	sīr fhalek!	سير فحالك!
Thief!	sheffar!	شفار!
Fire!	lᶜafīya!	العافية!
Danger	khâtâr	خطر
Help me please!	ᶜawennī ᶜafak!	عاوني عفاك!
Emergency!	'mestaᶜzhel!	مستعجل!
Where's the toilet?	fīn kein lbīt lma?	فين كان البيت الماء؟
I'm lost	tweḍḍert	توضرت

Can I use the telephone?
wakha nstaᶜmel ttīlīfūn? — واش نستعمل التليفون؟

I've lost my ...	tweḍḍer līya (m) ...	توضر لي . . .
	tweḍḍeraṭ līya (f) ...	توضرت لي . . .
	tweḍḍerū līya (pl) ...	توضرو لي . . .
daughter	bentī	بنتي
son	weldī	ولدي
bags	lhwayezh	الحوايج
handbag	ssak	ساك
money	lflūs	الفلوس
passport	lpaspūr	الباسبور
travellers cheques	shīkat seyahīya	شيكات سياحية
wallet	bezṭām	بزطام

There's been an accident!

ūqᶜat ksīda! وقعت كسيدة!

Call a doctor!

ᶜayyeṭ ᶜla shī ṭbīb! عيط علي شي طبيب!

Call an ambulance!

ᶜayyeṭ ᶜla ssayyara del'asᶜaf! عيط علي السيارة دال اسعاف!

I have medical insurance.

ᶜandī lasūrans dyal ṣṣhha عندي لاسورانس ديال الصحة

I'm ill.

ana mreiḍ (m) انا مريض

ana mreiḍa (f) انا مريضة

Contact (next of kin).

ttaṣel b (shī wahed men lᶜā'īla) تصل ب شي واحد من العاءلة

I'll call the police!

ghādī nᶜeyyaṭ ᶜla lbūlīs! غادي نعيط علي البوليس!

Call the police!

ᶜayyeṭ ᶜla lbūlīs! عيط علي البوليس!

Where's the police station?

fīn keina lkumesarīya? فين كاينة الكوميساريا؟

Someone robbed me!

serqna shī wahed! سرقني شي واحد!

DEALING WITH THE POLICE

My ... was stolen.	tesreq līya ... dyalī	تسرق لي . . . ديالي
bags	shshwaksh	شواكش
handbag	ssak	ساك
money	lflūs	الفلوس
papers/documents	lweraq	وراق
passport	lpaspōr	لباسبور
travellers cheques	shekat ssīyahī	الشيكات السياحية
wallet	lbezṭām	لبزطام

I've been assaulted/raped.
thzhem ʿlīya/ghtaṣabunī — تهجم علي / غتصبوني

I've been robbed.
tsreqt — تسرقت

I didn't do anything.
madert walū — مادرت والو

We're innocent.
hna 'abrīya'a — حنا ابرياء

I want to call my embassy/consulate.
bghīt nʿeyyet l ssīfara/ lkunsūlīya — بغيت نعيط علي السفارة / القنصلية

Can I call someone?
wash yemkenlī nʿeyyet tiltifūn? — واش يمكن لي نعيط علي واحد ؟

I want a lawyer who speaks English.
bghīṭ wahed lmuhamī llī keitkellem neglīzīya — بغيت واحد المحامي الي كيتكلم انكليزية

EMERGENCIES

GROWL!

When ʿ comes before a vowel, the vowel is 'growled' from the back of the throat. If it's before a consonant or at the end of a word, it sounds like a glottal stop.

I understand.
fhemt — فهمت

I don't understand.
mafhemtsh — مافهمتش

I'm sorry, forgive me.
smeh līya — سمح لي

I've been arrested.
thebst — تحبست

What am I accused of?
bash mthūm? — باش متهم؟

cell	lbenniqa	لبنيكة
jail	hebs	الحبس
judge	qadī	قاضي
guilty	mthūm	متهم
not guilty	barī	باريء
lawyer	muhamī	محامي
police officer	bulīsī	بوليسي
police station	kumīsarīya	كميسارية
prison	hebs	حبس
murder	qtīla	قتيلا
rape	ighteṣāb	اغتصاب
stealing	serqa	سرقة
traffic violation	khṭīya	خطية
trial	hukem	حكم
working without authorisation	khadem bla lwuraq	خادم بلا الوراق

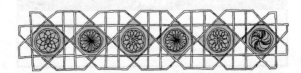

A

able (can)	qder	قدر
above	fuq	فوق
abroad	kharezh	الخارج
to accept	qbel	قبل
accident	ksīda	كسيدة
accommodation	'iqama	إقامة
across	qbalt	قبلت
address	ʿunwunʹ	عنوان
to admire	qedder	قدر
admission	'iʿtiraf	اعتراف
to admit	ʿtarf	اعترف
adult	balgh	البالغ
advantage	mzīya	مزية
advice	nāṣīha	نصيحة
aeroplane	ṭeiyāra	طيارة
after	men bʿd	من بعد
after-shave	rīha	ريحة
afternoon	ʿshīya	عشية
again	ʿawed tanī	عاودتاني
against	ḍeḍ	ضد
age	ʿmer	عمر
aggressive	wʿer	واعر
to agree	ttafq	اتفق
Agreed! mtafqīn!		متفقين
agriculture	fīlaha	فلاحة
ahead	qeddam	قدام
aid (help)	ʿawen	عون
AIDS	sīda	سيدا
air	hwa	هواء
air-conditioning	klīmatī-zasīyun	كليماتيزسيون
air mail	betteiyāra	بالطيارة
airport	maṭār	مطار
airport tax	darība dyal maṭār	ضريبة ديال المطار
alarm clock	feyyaq	الفياق
all	kūlshī	كول شي
allergy	hasasīya	حساسية
to allow	smeh	سمح
almost	tqrīban	تقريبا
alone	būwhedī	بوحدي
already	bʿda	بعد
also	htta	حتي
altitude	ʿulu	العلو
always	dīma	ديما
amateur	hawī	هاوي
ambassador	safīr	سفير
America	amrīka	امريكا
among	bīn	بين
ancient	qdīm	قديم
and	ū-	او
angry	ghedban	غضبان
animal	hayawan	حيوان
annual	ʿam l ʿam	عام ل عام
another one	wahed akhūr	واحد اخور
answer (n)	zhawab	جواب
ant	nemla	نملة
antibiotics	'antībīyutik	انتيبيوتيك
antique	ʿareq	عريق
any	shī	شي
apple	teffah	تفاح
appointment	mīʿad	ميعاد
approximately	tqrīban	تقريبا
archaeology	ʿlīm dyal latar	علم ديال الاثار
architect	muhendīs	مهندس
architecture	handasa	هندسة
to argue	tkhaṣem	تخاصم
arm	draʿ	دراع
around	zhwayeh	جوايح
arrival	wṣul	وصول
to arrive	wṣel	وصل
art	fenn	فن
artist	fennan	فنان
ashtray	tfaya	طفاية
to ask	sewwel	سول
asleep	naʿes	ناعس
aspirin	asprīn	اسبيرين
atmosphere	zhew	الجو
aunt (paternal)	ʿemma	عمة
(maternal)	khala	خالة
Australia	astrālīya	استراليا
autumn (fall)	khrīf	خريف

avenue	sharīᶜ	شاريع
awake	fayeq	فايق
awful	khayb	خايب

B

baby	derri ṣghīr	دري صغير
baby food	makla dyal drari sghar	مكلة ديال ردراري صغار
babysitter	murabbiya dyal drari sghar	ربية ديال م درادي صغار
back	lōr	لور
back (body)	ḍher	ضهر
backpack	sakaḍō	ساكاضو
bad	khaib	خايب
bag	khensha	خنشة
bag	sak	ساك
baggage	bagazh	باكاج
bakery	ferran	فران
balcony	balkōn	بلكون
ball	kura	كرة
ballet	qurṭasa	قرطسة
banana	banan	بنان
band (music)	mezhmuᶜ	مجموعة
bandage	faṣma	فاصمة
bank	bānka	بنك
barber	hellaq	حلاق
basket	sella	سلة
bath	hemmam	حمام
bathing suit	mayyu	مايو
bathroom	bīt lma	بيت الماء
bathtub	hemmam	حمام
battery	batrī	بتري
beach	laplazh	لابلاج
beans (green)	lūbīya	لوبية
beautiful	zwīn	زوين
because	ᶜla qībal	علي قبال
bed	namūsīya	نموسية
bedroom	bīt nnᶜas	بيت نعاس
bee	nehla	نحلة
beef	begrī	بكري
beer	bīra	بيرا

before	qbel	قبل
beggar	ṭallab	طلاب
to begin	bda	بدأ
behind	mura	مورا
below	teht	تحت
beside	zhenb	جنب
best	rfeᶜ	رفيع
to bet	tkhater	تخاتر
better	hessen	حسن
between	ma bīn	مابين
bicycle	beshklīṭā	بشكليطة
big	kbīr	كبير
bill	faktūra	فكتورة
binoculars	shūwafat	شوفات
bird	ṭeir	طير
birth certificate	ᶜaqed līzdiyad	عقد لزدياد
birthday	ᶜīd lmīlad	عيد الميلاد
biscuits	helwat	حلوة
bite	ᶜeḍḍa	عضة
to bite	ᶜeḍḍ	عض
black	khel	كحل
blanket	bṭṭānīya	بطانية
to bleed	seyyel ddemm	سيل الدم
to bless	rHem	رحم
blind	ᶜma	عمي
blood	demm	الدم
blood group	nnuᶜ dyal ddemm	نوع ديال الدم
blood test	duwwez ddemm	دوز الدم
blue	zerq	زرق
boat	flūka	فلوكة
body	zhesm	جسم
to boil	sleq	سلق
boiled	mslūq	مسلوق

Bon appétit!
besha ū rraha — بصحة و راحة

Bon voyage!
ṭrīq ssalama — طريق السلامة

bone	ᶜḍem	عضم
book	ktab	كتاب
bookshop	mektaba	مكتبة

boots	butīyun	بوتيو
border	hdada	حدود
bored	meqnuṭ	مقنوط
boring	mqnat	مقناط
to borrow	tsellef	تسلف
both	bzhūzh	ب جوج
bottle	qerᶜa	قرعة
bottle opener	lfttaha	الفتاحة
boulevard	sharīᶜ	شاريع
bowl	zlafa	زلفة
box	senduq	صندوق
box (cardboard)	kartūna	كرطونة
boxing	lbōks	بوكس
boy	weld	ولد
boyfriend	saheb	صاحب
bracelet	deblīzh	دبليج
brass	nhas ṣfer	نحاس اصفر
brave	shzhīᶜ	شجيع
bread	khūbz	خبز
to break	herres	هرس
breakable	īqder ītherres	اقدراتهرس
breakfast	fṭur	فطور
to breathe	nfes	نفس
bribe	reshwa	رشوة
bridge	qenṭra	قنطرة
to bring	zhīb	جيب
broken	mherres	مهرس
broom	sheṭṭāba	شطابة
brother	akh	اخ
brown	qehwī	قهوي
to bruise	tqesseh	تقصح
brush	shīta	شيتا
bucket	sṭel	سطل
Buddhist	būḍī	بودي
bug	hashara	حشرة
to build	bnī	بني
building	bnī	البني
burn	herqa	حريق
bus (city)	ṭōbīs	طوبيس
bus (intercity)	kar	كار
bus station	meheṭṭa	محطة
bus stop	blaṣa dyal ṭṭōbīsat	بلكة ديال الطوبيسات
business	tizhara	تجارة
businessperson	tazher	تاجر
busy	meshghūl	مشغول
but	walakīn	ولكن
butter	zebda	زبدة
butterfly	fertattu	فرتاتو
buttermilk	lben	لبن
buttons	ṣḍāf	صضاف
to buy	shrī	شري

C

cabbage	krum	كروم
calendar	yawmīya	يومية
calm	hanī	هاني
camel	zhmel	جمل
camera	ṣṣuwwara	صورة
camera shop	ssuwwar	صوار
to camp	khiyyem	خيم
campsite	mukhayyam	مخيم
can (aluminium)	huk	حوك
can (be able)	qder	قدر
can opener	hellala	حلالة
Canada	kanada	كند
to cancel	lgha	لغ
candle	shmaᶜa	شمعة
car	ṭumubīl	طموبيل
cards	karta	كرط
care (about)	htam	هتم

Careful!
redd balek! رد بالك

carpet	zerbīya	زربية
to carry	hez	هز
carton	karṭōn	كرطون
cashier	mzher dyal flūs	مجر ديال الفلوس
cassette	kassīṭ	كسيت
castle	qṣer	قصر
cat	meshsh	مش
cave	ghar	غار
to celebrate	htafel	احتفل
centimetre	ṣāntīm	سنتيم
ceramic	zhellizh	جليج
certificate	shhada	شهادة

chair	kūrsī	كرسي
chance	furṣa	فرصة
to change	ṣerref	صرف
change (coins)	ṣerf	صرف
cheap	rkheiṣ	رخيص
to cheat	gheshsh	غش
to check	qelleb	قلب
check-in (desk)	mektab dyal tszhīl	مكتب ديال التسجيل
cheese	frumazh	فرماج
chemist	lfārmasyan	الفرماسيان
chess	strunzh	سترنج
chest	sder	صدر
chewing gum	mska	مسكة
chicken	dzhazh	دجاج
child	derrī	دري
children	drerri	دراري
chocolate	sheklāṭ	شكلات
to choose	khtar	ختار
Christian	masīhī	مسيحي
church	kanīsa	كنيسة
cigarettes	garru	كارو
cinema	sīnīma	سينما
circus	sīrk	سيرك
citizenship	zhensīya	جنسية
city	mdīna	مدينة
city centre	wuṣṭ lmdīna	وسط المدينة
civil rights	qanūn lmadanī	قانون المدني
class	qsem	قسم
clean	nqī	نقي
to clean	neddef	نضف
clear (understood)	ṣāfī	صافي
client	klīyan	كليان
cliff	skher	صخر
to climb	tleᶜ	اطلع
clock	magana	ماكانة
to close	sedd	سد
closed	mesdūd	مسدود
clothing	hawayzh	حوايج
clothing store	mahal dyal lhawayzh	محل ديال الحوايج

cloud	ḍbaba	ضباب
coast	muhīṭ	محيط
coat	kbōṭ	كبوط
coffee	qehwa	قهوة
coins	ṣerf	صرف
coke	kōka	كوكا
cold (adj)	bared	بارد
cold (illness)	mrewweh	مروح
cold water	lma bared	الماه بارد
colleague	zmīl	زميل
college	zhamīᶜ	جامعة
colour	lūn	لون
comb	meshṭa	مشطة
come!	azhī!	اجي!
come	zha	جا
comedy	frazha	فرجة
comfortable	mreyyeh	مريح
comics	nukat	نكات
commerce	tīzhara	تجارة
companion	sahb	صاحب
company	sharīka	شركة
compass	bōṣala	بوصلة
complaint	shekwa	شكوة
computer	muhasīb	محاسب
concert	shra	سهرة
confirm (booking)	hzhez	حجز
congratulations	mbrūk	مبروك
conservative	muhafīd	محافظ
constipation	tᶜsam	تعصام
construction work	bnī	البني
consulate	qusūlīya	قنصلية
contact lenses	ᶜadasat dyal shshūf	عدسات ديال الشوف
contraceptives	dwa ded lhmel	دوي ضد الحمل
contract	kuntra	كونطرا
cook	tbakh	طباخ
to cook	ṭeyyeb	طيب
copper	nhas hmer	نحاس احمر
corner	qent	قنت
corrupt	reshwī	رشاوي

cost	taman	ثمن
to cost	swa	سوي
cotton	qten	قطن
cough	keha	كحة
to count	hseb	حسب
country	blad	بلاد
country market	sūq	سوق
countryside	badīya	بادية
coupon	bun	البون
court (legal)	mhkama	محكمة
(tennis)	tīran dyal tinīs	تران ديال تنيس
cow	begra	بكرة
crafty	hraymī	حرايمي
crazy	hemq	حمق
credit card	kart krīdī	كارت كريدي
cross-country trail	rīf	ريف
cross (angry)	k'a	كعا
crossroad	kerwazma	كروزمة
crowded	zham	زحام
cup	kas	كاس
curtain	khamīya	خامية
customs	'adat	عادات
customs official	dīwānī	ديواني
to cut	qṭ'	قطع

D

dad	bba	با
daily	yawmīyyan	يوميا
damp	fazeg	فازك
to dance	shṭeh	شطح
dancing	shṭīh	شطيح
dangerous	khāṭār	خطر
dark	ḍlem	ضلم
dark (colour)	meghlūq	مغلوق
date	tarīkh	تاريخ
date of birth	nhar zzīyada	نهار زيادة
daughter	bent	بنت
dawn	fzher	فجر
day	nhar	نهار
day after tomorrow	be'd ghedda	غدا بعد
day before yesterday	wel lbareh	اول بارح
dead	miyyet	ميت
deaf	smek	سمك
to deal	t'amel	تعامل
death	mūt	موت
to decide	qerrer	قرر
deep	ghareq	غارق
deer	kurkdan	كركدان
to delay	'ṭel	عطل
delicious	bnin	بنين
delirious	thaṭīr	تهاطير
democracy	dimūqāṭīya	دموقراطية
dentist	ṭbīb dyal ssnan	طبيب ديال السنان
to deny	refḍ	رفض
deodorant	rīha	ريحة
to depart	khrezh	خرج
departure	dahab	دهاب
descendent	men ssulala	من سلالة
desert	ṣehra	سحراء
destination	tīzhan	اتجاه
to destroy	heddem	هدم
detail	tefṣīl	تفاصيل
diabetic	fīh sukkar	فيه سكر
diaper	khruq	خروق
diarrhoea	kersh zharīya	جارية كرش
diary	mudakkīra	مدكرة
dictionary	munzhīd	منجد
to die	mat	مات
different	mekhtalef	مختلف
difficult	ṣ'eib	صعب
dinner	'sha	عشاء
direct	nīshan	نيشان
director	mudīr	مدير
dirt	trāb	طراب
dirty	mwessekh	موسخ
disabled	mu'ewweq	معوق
discount	tekhfīd	تخفيض

to discover	ktashef	كتشف
discrimination	ᶜunsurīya	عنصرية
disease	merḍa	مرضة
dismissal	merfōḍ	مرفوض
dizzy	dūkha	دوخة
to do	dar	دار
doctor	ṭbīb	طبيب
documentary	wataᶜīq	وتايق
dog	kelb	كلب
doll	munīka	منيكة
donkey	hmar	حمار
door	bab	باب
double	zhuzh	جوج
double bed	srīr dyal zhuzh	سرير ديال جوج
double room	bīt dyal zhuzh	بيت ديال جوج
dozen	zīna	زنة
drama	maᶜsat	مأسات
to dream	hlem	حلم
dress	keswa	كسوة
to dress	lbes	لبس
to drink	shreb	شرب
to drive	ṣāg	ساق
driver's licence	permī	برمي
to drop	ṭeyyeh	طيح
drugs	mukhdīrat	مخدرات
drum	ṭbel	طبل
drunk (adj)	sekran	سكران
dry (adj)	nashef	ناشف
to dry	nshef	نشف
dull	hafī	حافي
dummy (pacifier)	skata	سكاة
dust	ghubra	غبرة
duty	wazheb	واجب

E

each (one)	kūl wahed	كل واحد
ear	wden	ودن
early	bekrī	بكري
to earn	rbeh	ربح
earrings	twaneg	طوانك
ears	wednīn	ودنين
earth	denya	دنيا
earth (soil)	lerḍ	لرض
earthquake	zelzla	زلزال
east	sherq	شرق
easy	sahel	سهل
to eat	kla	كلي
Eat! kūl!		كول!
economic	qtīṣādī	اقتصادي
economy	qtīṣad	اقتصاد
editor	nashīr	ناشر
educated	qarī	قاريء
education	teᶜlīm	تعلم
eggs	beiḍ	بيض
election	intīkhab	انتخاب
electricity	ḍu	ضو
elevator	sansūr	سنسور
embarassed	hshem	حشم
embarassment	hshūma	حشومة
embassy	sīfāra	السفارة
embroidery	ṭerz	طرز
emergency	mustaᶜzhel	مستعجل
employee	kheddam	خدام
employer	baṭrōn	بترون
empty	khawī	خاوي
end	akher	اخر
engagement	muwafaqat zzawazh	موافقة الزواج
engine	muṭōr	مطور
engineer	mūhendīs	مهندس
engineering	handasa	هندسة
England	anglatīra	انكلترا
English	neglīzīya	انكلنزي
enjoy (oneself)	nsheṭ ᶜla rasek	نشط علي راسك
enough	kafī	كافي
enter	dkhel	دخل
entertaining	tenshīṭ	تنشيط
entrance	dekhla	دخلة
envelope	zhwa	جوي
environment	bīᶜa	بيئة
epilepsy	larīh	لرياح
equal	bhal bhal	بحال بحال

equipment	tezhīz	تجهيز
essential	ḍarurī	ضروري
Europe	ūruba	اوروبا
European	ūrubī	اوروبي
even so		
wekhkha dak shī		وخ داكشي
evening	ᶜshīya	عشية
every day	kūl nhar	كل نهار
everything	kūl shī	كولشي
exact	huwa hadak	هو هدك
example	mītal	متل
excellent	rfīᶜ	رفيع
exchange	tebdīl	تبديل
exchange rate		
qīma dyal ṣṣerf		قيمة ديال الصرف
excluded	mṭruḍ	مطرود
excuse (n)	ᶜḍer	عدر
Excuse me.		
smeh līya		سمح لي
to exhibit	ᶜerḍ	عرض
exhibition	ᶜarḍ	عرض
exit	khurouzh	الخروج
expensive	ghalī	غالي
experience	tezhrība	تجربة
exploitation	ᶜistighlal	استغلال
express	sarīᶜ	سريع
express mail		
lbared lᶜazhīl		البريد العاجل
extra	zayed	زايد
eye	ᶜeyn	عين

F

fabric	tūb	توب
face	wzheh	وجه
factory	mᶜmel	معمل
to faint	skhef	سخف
fair	mnaseb	مناسب
fake	mzwwer	مزور
fall (autumn)	khrīf	الخريف
family	ᶜa'īla	عائلة
famous	mshhōr	مشهور
fan	reyyaha	رياحة
fans (of team)	muhīb	محب
far	bᶜeid	بعيد
farm	fīrma	فرمة
farmer	fellah	فلاح
fast (adj)	ḍghīya	دغي
to fast	ṣām	صام
fat	ghled	غليض
father	walīd	والد
father-in-law	nsīb	نسيب
faucet (tap)	rōbīnī	دوبيني
fault (someone's)	ghalaṭ	غلط
fear	khūf	خوف
to feel	hess	حس
feelings	ᶜihsas	احساس
fence	mukhliweḍ	مخلوض
festival	musem	موسم
fever	skhana	سخانة
few	qlīl	قليل
fiancée/fiancé	khaṭīb/ khatība	خطيب / خطيبة
fiction	khayalī	خيالي
field (land)	'erḍ	الارض
to fight	ḍḍarb	ضارب
to fill	ᶜammer	عمر
film	fīlm	فيلم
filtered	mṣeffī	مصفي
to find	lga	لكا
fine	zwīn	زوين
finger	ṣbeᶜ dyal yeddᶜ	صبع ديال اليد
Finish!		
kemmel!		كمل !
fire	ᶜafīya	عافية
firewood	hṭeb	حطب
first	luwwel	للول
fish	hōt	حوت
fish shop	hanūt dyal lhōṭ	لحانوت اديال الحوت
flag	raya	راية
flashlight	pīl	بيل
flat (land, etc)	waṭīya	واطية

flea	beq	بق
flight	ṭeiyara	طيارة
floor	'erḍ	الارض
floor (storey)	ṭebqa	طبقة
flour	dgīg	دكيك
flower	werḍa	وردة
flower seller	mūl lwerḍ	مو الورد
to fly	ṭār	طار
fly (insect)	debbana	دبانة
follow	tbeᶜ	تبع
food	makla	مكلة
foot	rzhel	رجل
football (soccer)	kōra	الكرة
footpath	mrīra	مريرة
foreign	azhnabī	اجنبي
foreigner	azhnabī	اجنبي
forest	ghaba	غابة
forever	dīma	ديما
to forget	nsa	نسي
to forgive	smeh	سمح
fork	fershetta	فرشطة
fortnight	kanza	الكانزة
fortune teller	shuwwaf	شواف
fountain	khᶜṣṣa	خصة
fourth	rūbūᶜ	ربع
free (not busy)	msalī	مسالي
free (of charge)	fābōr	فابور
freedom	hurrīya	حرية
to freeze	tellezh	تلج
fresh	ṭrei	طري
Friday	zhzhemᶜa	الجمعة
fried	meqlī	مقلي
friend	ṣāheb	صاحب
front	qeddam	قدام
frozen foods		
makla mtelzha		مكلة متلجة
fruit	fakīya	فاكية
full	ᶜamer	عامر
fun	nashāṭ	نشاط
funeral	gnaza	كنازة
future	mūsteqbal	مستقبل

G

game	leᶜba	لعبة
garage	garazh	كراج
garbage	zbel	ذبل
garden	zharda	جردة
gardening	teswab dyal zherda	تصواب ديال الجردة
garlic	tūma	تومة
gas cartridge	bōṭa dyal lgaz	بوطة ديال الكاز
gate	bab	باب
general	ᶜamm	عام
germ	mīkrūb	مكروب
German	almanī	الماني
Germany	almanīya	المانية
Get lost!		
sīr fehalek!		سير ف حالك!
gift	hdīya	هدية
girl	bent	بنت
girlfriend	ṣahba	صاحبة
to give	ᶜṭa	عط
glass	zhazh	جاج
glass (drinking)	kas	كاس
glasses (eye)	nḍāder	نظادر
glue	lṣāq	لساق
to go	msha	مشي
go away	sīr fhalek	سر فحالك
Go straight ahead.		
sīr nīshan		سر نيشان
goal	hadaf	هدف
goat	meᶜza	معزة
God	llah	الله
gold	dheb	دهب
good	mezyan	مزيان
goodbye	bessalama	بسلامة
government	hūkūma	حكومة
gram	gram	كرام
grandchild	hafīd	حفيد
grandfather	zhedd	الجد
grandmother	zhedda	الجدة

DICTIONARY

grape	ʿneb	عنب
grass	rbīʿ	ربيع
grave	qbur	قبر
Great!		
bikhīr!		بخير!
green	khḍer	خضر
greengrocer	mul lkhuḍra	مول الخضرة
grey	rmadī	رمادي
guardian	ʿssas	عساس
to guess	qedder	قدر
guest	ḍeif	ضيف
guide (n)	gīd	كيد
guitar	gīṭar	كيطار
gum	mska	مسكة
gym	qaʿa dyal rīyaḍa	قاعة ديال الرياضة
gymnastics	rīyaḍa	رياضة

H

habit	ʿada	عادة
hair	shʿr	شعر
hairbrush	meshta dyal shshʿar	مشطة ديال الشعر
half	neṣṣ	نص
hammer	mṭerqa	مطرقة
hand	yedd	يد
handbag	sak	صاك
handicrafts	harayfīya	حريفية
handmade	belyedd	باليد
handsome	zwīn	زوين
happy	ferhan	فرحان
harbour	merṣa	مرسي
hard	qaṣeh	قاصح
harass	shṭen	شطن
hat	terbūsh	طربوش
have	ʿand	عند
he	huwwa	هو
head	rāṣ	الراس
headache	hrīq raṣ	حريق راس
health	ṣehha	صحة
hear	smeʿ	سمع
hearing aid	semmaʿa	سماعة
heart	qelb	قلب
heat	ṣehḍ	صهد
heater	sekhkhana	سخانة
heavy	tqīl	ثقيل
Hello! (answering telephone)		
alō		آلو
Hello.		
labas		لاباس
helmet	kask	كاسك
help	mūsaʿada	مساعدة
to help	ʿawen	عاون
Help me!		
ʿawennī!		عاوني!
herbalist	ʿashshab	عشاب
herbs	ʿazhūb	العشوب
here	hna	هنا
high	ʿalī	عالي
high school	tanawī	الثانوي
hill	tal	تل
Hindu	hendī	هندي
hire (rent)	kra	كراء
historical ruins	ʾatar	الاثار
hitchhike	luṭusṭub	لطسطب
hole	teqbu	تقبة
holiday	ʿuṭla	عطلة
homeless	msherred	المشرد
honest	mʿqūl	معقول
honey	ʿsel	عسل
horrible	khayeb	خايب
horse	ʿawd	العود
horse riding	rkub lkhīl	ركوب الخيل
hospital	ṣbīṭār	سبيطار
hot	skhūn	سخون
hot (spicy)	harr	حار
hot water	lma skhūn	لما سخون
hotel	ūṭeil	لوتيل
hour	saʿa	ساعة
house	dar	دار
housework	khedma dyal ddar	خدمة ديال الدار
How?		
kīfash?		كفاش؟

H

DICTIONARY

hug	ʿenneq	عنق
human rights	huqq lʿinsan	حق الانسان
hundred	mya	ميي
hungry	zhīʿan	جعان
Hurry up!		
serbī!		سربي !
husband	razhel	رجل

I

ice	telzh	تلج
ice cream	laglas	لكلاس
idea	fikra	فكرة
identification	teʿrīf	تعريف
identification card	biṭaqa ttaʿrīf	بطاقة تعريف
if	ila	إلا
ill	mrīḍḍ	مريض
immediately	fissaʿ	فساع
immigration	hizhra	هجرة
important	muhimm	مهم
industry	sinaʿa	صناعة
information	meʿlūmat	معلومات
inject	hqen	حقن
injection	shūka	شوكة
injury	zherha	جرحة
inside	dakhel	لداخل
inspector	mūfettīsh	مفتش
instructor	murshīd	مرشد
insurance	lāṣurānṣ	لصورنس
intense	shdīd	شديد
interesting	mūhī	مهم
intermission	istiraha	استراحة
international	ʿalamī	عالمي
interview	istezhwab	اسستجواب
island	zhazīra	جزيرة
itch (n)	hkka	حكة
itinerary	ṭrīq	طريق

J

jacket	kebbuṭ	كبوت
jail	hebs	حبس
jam	kufitir	كوفيتير
jar	gherraf	غراف
jealous	hessad	حساد
jeans	dzhzhin	دجين
jewellery	bīzhū	بيجو
Jewish	ihudī	ايهودي
job (work)	khedma	خدمة
joke	nekta	نكتة
to joke	ḍhek	ضحك
journalist	ṣāhāfī	صحافي
journey	safar	سفر
judge	qaḍī	قاضي
juice	ʿaṣeir	عصير
to jump	nqez	نقز
Just a minute.		
wahed dqīqa		واحد دقيقة
justice	ʿeḍala	عدالة

K

key	sarūt	ساروت
keyboard	ʿaddad	العداد
to kick	rkel	ركل
to kill	qtel	قتل
kilogram	kīlū	كيلو
kilometre	kīlūmīter	كيلومتر
kind	ḍrīf	طريف
king	malik	ملك
kiss	būsa	بوسة
to kiss	bas	باس
kitchen	kūzīna	كوزينة
kitten	mshīsha	مشيشة
knapsack	ṣakaḍō	صاك آضو
knee	rekba	ركبة
knife	mūs	موس
to knock	deqq	دق
to know	ʿref	عرف

L

lace	sīr	سير
lake	ḍaya	ضاية
lamb	ghenmī	غنمي
land	ʼerḍ	ارض

language	lūgha	لغة
large	kbīr	كبير
last (final)	akhīr	اخير
late	mᶜeṭṭel	معطل
to laugh	ḍhek	ضحك
launderette	meṣbana	مصبنة
law	qanūn	قانون
lawyer	mūhamī	محامي
lay down		
tekka		تقة
lazy	fenyan	فنيان
leader	raᶜis	ريس
learn	tᶜellem	تعلم
leather	zheld	جلد
left (not right)	līser	ليسر
leg	rzhel	رجل
legalisation	muwafaq	موفق
lemon	hameḍ	حامض
length	ṭul	طول
lens	zhzha	الجاجة
less	qell	قل
Let's go.		
yallah		يالاه
letter	bra	برا
liar	keddab	كذاب
library	khīzana	خزانة
lice	gmel	كمل
to lie	kdeb	كذب
life	hayat	حياة
lift (elevator)	sensūr	سنسور
light (sun/lamp)	ḍu	ضو
(weight)	khfīf	خفيف
(colour)	meftūh	مفتوح
light bulb	bula	بولة
like (similar)	bhal	بحال
to like	bgha	بغ
line	sherṭa	شرطة
lips	shlaqem	شلاقم
lipstick	ᶜker	لعكر
listen	smeᶜ	سمع
little (amount)	qlīl	قليل
(small)	shwīya	شوي
little bit		
shī shwīya		شي شوي
live (somewhere)	saken	ساكن
local	mahalī	محلي
location	mawqiᶜ	موقع
lock	qfel	قفل
to lock	sedd	سد
long	ṭwīl	طويل
to look	shaf	شاف
Look!		
shūf!		شوف!
loose	metlūq	مطلوق
loose change	ṣṣerf	صرف
lose	twedder	توضر
loser	khaser	خاسر
loss	khesran	خسران
lost	talf	تالف
loud	mzhehhed	مجهد
love	hebb	حب
lover	hbīb	حبيب
low	habṭ	هابط
loyal	ṣadīq	صادق
luck	zher	زهر
luggage	hwayezh	حوايج
lump	kutla	كتلة
lunch	ghda	غدا
lunchtime	weqt lgheda	وقت الغدا
luxury	rafahīya	رفاهية

M

machine	makīna	ماكينة
mad	mṣeṭṭī	مصطي
made (of)	mesnūᶜ men	مصنوع من
magazine	mazhella	مجلة
magician	sehhar	سحار
mail	bared	بريد
mailbox	sendūq dyal lbrawat	صندوق ديال البروات
mailman	faktur	فكتور
majority	aghlabīya	اغلبنة

make-up	tezhmīl	تجميل
make	ṣaweb	صوب
make fun of ḍhek 'la		ضحك علي
male	dker	دكر
man	razel	راجل
manager	musayyer	مسير
many	bezzaf	بزاف
map	kharīta	خريطة
market	sūq	سوق
marriage	zwazh	زواج
married	mzewwezh	مزوج
to marry	zuwwezh	زوج
marvellous	ʿazhīb	عجيب
mat	hṣīra	حصيرة
matches	wqeid	وقيد
mattress	mḍerreba	مضربة
maybe	yemken	يمكن
meaning	meʿna	معني
meat	lhem	لحم
mechanic	mikanīsiyan	ميكانيسيان
medal	midaya	مداية
medicine	dwa	دواء
to meet	tlaqa mʿa	تلق مع
member	ʿuḍō	عضو
menstruation	weqt ddemm	وقت الدم
menu	wezhba	وجبة
message	mīṣāzh	مساج
metal	ṣulb	صلب
metre	mītrū	مترو
midnight	tnash dllīl	تناش دليل
migraine	shqīqa	شقيقة
military	ʿaskarīya	عسكرية
milk	hlīb	حليب
millimetre	milmeter	ململتر
million	melyūn	مليون
mind	ʿqel	عقل
mineral water	lma maʿdīnī	ماء معدنية
mint tea	'atī benna'naʿ	اتاي بنعنع
minute	dqīqa	دقيقة
mirror	mraya	مراية

miss (feel absence)	twehhesh	توحش
mistake	ghalṭa	غلطة
to mix	khelleṭ	خلط
moisturising cream	dhna dyal luwzhih	دهنة ديال الوجه
money	flūs	فلوس
monkey	qerd	قرد
month	shher	شهر
monument	atar	آتار
moped	muṭur	موتور
moon	gmra	قمر
more	kter	كتر
morning	ṣbah	صباح
mosque	zhameʿ	جامع
mother	walīda	والدة
mother-in-law	nsība	نسيبة
motorcycle	muṭur	موتور
mountain	zhbel	جبل
mountain range	silsila dyal zhzhbal	سلسلة ديال جبال
mouse	far	فار
mouth	fūmm	فم
movie	fīlm	فلم
mud	ghīs	غيس
mule	bghel	بغل
Mum	mmī	مي
muscle	ʿadala	عضلة
museum	methef	متحف
music	mūsīqa	موسيقي
musician	musīqar	موسيقار
Muslim	meslem	مسلم
mute	zanzōn	زنزون
mutton	ghenm	غنمي

N

name	smīya	سمي
nappy	khruq	خروق
nationality	zhensīya	جنسية
nature	ṭabīyʿa	طبيعة
near	qrīb	قريب
necessary	lazem	لازم

necklace	sensla	سنسلة
to need	htazh	حتاج
needle (sewing)	ībra	ابرا
(syringe)	ībra	ابرا
neighbour	zhar	جار
neither	hetta wahed	حتي واحد
net	shebka	شبكة
never	ʿemmer	عمر
new	zhdīd	جديد
news	khbar	اخبار
newsagency	wakalat lkhbar	وكالة الاخبار
newspaper	zharīda	جريدة
next	zhay	جاي
next to	hda	حدا
nice	zwīn	زوين
night	līla	ليلا
no	la	لا
nobody	hetta wahed	حتي واحد
noise	ṣḍaʿ	صداع
noisy	kein ṣḍaʿ	كاين صداع
none	walū	والو
noon	weṣṭ nnhar	وسط النهار
north	shamal	شمال
nose	nīf	نيف
nosey	fḍulī	فضولي
not	mashī	ماشي
not yet	mazal	مازال
notebook	karnī	كرني
nothing	walū	والو
novel (book)	qeṣṣa	قصة
now	daba	دبا
number	raqem	رقم
nurse	fermlīya	فرمليا

O

obvious	bayn	باين
ocean	bhar	بحر
of	dyal	ديال
offence	mukhalafa	مخالفة
office	mektab	مكتب
often	bezzaf	بزاف
oil	zīt	زيت
OK	wakha	واخ
old	qdım	قديم
old city mdīna qdīma		مدينة قديمة
olive	zītūn	زيتون
olive oil	zīt lʿūd	زيت زيتون
on	ʿla	علي
on time	felweqt	في الوقت
once	merra	مرة
one-way (ticket)	mshī	مشي
only	ghīr	غير
open (adj)	mehlūl	محلول
to open	hell	حل
operation (surgery)	ʿamalīya	عملية
operator	teqnī	تقني
opinion	fikra	فكرة
opposite	ʿeks	عكس
or	'ūlla	الا
oral	belheḍra	بالهضرة
orange	līmūn	ليمون
orange (colour)	līmūnī	ليموني
orchestra	ūrkestra	اركسترا
order	ṭālāb	طلب
to order	ṭleb	طلب
ordinary	ʿadī	عادي
organise	neḍḍem	نظم
original	'eṣlī	اصلي
other	akhūr	اخر
outside	berra	برا
over	fūq men	فوق من
overcoat	munṭu	منطو
owe	tsal	تسال
owner	mul	مول
oxygen	hwa	هوا

P

pacifier (dummy)	skata	سقتة
package	bakīya	بكية
padlock	qfel	قفل
page	ṣefha	صفحة

O

DICTIONARY

P

pain	luzheᶜ	لوجع
painful	kayder	كيضر
paint	ṣbagha	صباغة
to paint	ṣbegh	صبغ
paint (pictures)	rsem	رسم
painter	ṣebbagh	صباغ
paintings	teṣawer	تصور
pair (a couple)	ferda	فردة
palace	qṣer	قصر
pan	meqla	مقلة
pants	serwal	سروال
paper	werqa	ورقة
paper (wrapping)	kaghīt	كاغيط
parcel	kūlīya	كلية
parents	walidīn	والدين
park	ṣaha	ساحة
to park	wqef	وقف
part	ṭerf	طرف
party (fiesta)	hefla	حفلة
party (politics)	hīzab	حزب
passenger	muṣafīr	مسافر
passport	pasbōr	باسبور
passport number	nemra dyal lpaspōr	نمرة ديال البسبور
past	māḍei	ماضي
path	ṭriq ṣghīr	طريق صغير
patient (adj)	ṣebbar	صبار
to pay	khelleṣ	خلص
payment	khlas	خلاص
peace	salam	سلام
peak	raṣ	راس
pedestrian	balīd	بليد
pen	stīlū	ستيلو
penalty	khṭeiya	خطية
pencil	qalam	قلم
penknife	mūs	موس
people	nas	ناس
pepper	lebzār	لبزار
percent	felmya	فالمية
performance	dawer	دور
perfume	rīha	ريحة
permanent	dīma	ديما
permission	rūkhsa	رخصة
personal	shekhsī	شخصي
personality	shekhsīya	شخصية
perspire	ᶜreq	عرق
petition	lmūzheb	لموجب
petrol	līṣanṣ	لسانس
pharmacy	farmasyan	فرمسيان
phone book	ktab dyal tīlīfōn	كتاب ديال التليفون
phone box	dalīl dyal tīlīfōn	تليفون عمومي
photo	teṣwīra	تصويرة
photographer	muṣawwer	مصور
photography	tṣwir	تصوير
to pick up	hezz	هز
picture	teṣwīra	تصويرة
piece	ṭerf	طرف
pig	hellūf	حللوف
pill	fanīda	فنيدة
pillow	mkhedda	مخدة
pillowcase	ghesha dyal lmkhedda	غسنا ديال المخدة
pink	fanīdī	فنيدي
pipe	tīyyū	تييو
pitcher	ghurraf	غراف
place	blāṣa	بلاصة
plain	ᶜadī	عادي
plane	ṭiyyara	طيارة
planet	kewkeb	كوكب
plant	ghers	غرس
to plant	ghers	غرس
plastic	mīkka	ميكة
plate	ṭebṣīl	طبسل
play (theatre)	temtīl	تمتيل
to play	lᶜeb	لعب
player (sports)	laᶜb	لعاب
playing cards	karta	الكارطة
please	ᶜafak	عفاك
plug (bath)	gfala	قفلة
plug (electricity)	prīz	بريز
pocket	zhīb	جيب
poetry	shiᶜr	شعر
poison	semm	سم
police	būlīs	بوليس
policeman	būlīsī	بوليسي

DICTIONARY

police station	kumīsarīya	كميسارية
politician	sīyasī	سياسي
politics	sīyasīya	سياسة
pollution	talawuth	تلوث
pool (swimming)	pīsīn	بيسين
poor	meskīn	مسكين
popular	m'rūf	معروف
port	mersa	مرسي
possible	yemken	يمكن
post code	ramz lbaredī	الرمز البريدي
post office	busṭa	بوسطة
postage	irsal	ارسال
postcard	kart pustal	كارط بوستال
pot	ṭenzhra	طنجرة
potato	bṭāṭā	بطاطا
pottery	fekhkhar	فخار
poverty	faqer	فقير
power	sultṭa	ملطة
prayer	muṣllī	مصلي
to prefer	fḍel	فضل
pregnant	hamla	حاملة
to prepare	wzhzhed	وجد
prescription	werqa dyal ṭṭōbīb	ورقة ديال الطبيب
present (gift)	hdīya	هدية
present (time)	daba	داب
presentation	teqdīm	تقديم
president	ra'īs	رئيس
pressure	ḍeghṭ	ضغط
pretty	zwīn	زوين
prevent	mne'	منع
price	taman	تمن
pride	iftīkhar	افتخار
prime minister	wazīr luwwel	وزير الاول
prison	hebs	حبس
prisoner	hebbas	حباس
private	khaṣ	خاص
problem	mūshkīl	مشكل
profession	mihna	مهنة
profit	rbih	ربح
program	bernamezh	برنامج
promise	wa'd	وعد
pronunciation	nutq	نطق
proposal	iqtīrah	اقتراح
to protect	hfeḍ	حفض
protest	'areḍ	عارض
to pull	zhbed	جبد
pump	bumba	بومبة
puncture	teqba	تقبة
to punish	'qeb	عقب
puppy	klīyeb	كليب
pure	ṣāfī	صافي
purse	sak	ساك
to push	dfe'	دفع
to put	heṭṭ	حط

Q

quality	zhūda	جودة
quantity	'adad	عدد
to quarrel	dabez	دابز
queen	malīka	ملكة
question	sū'al	سوءال
to question	sewwel	سول
quick	zerba	زربة
quickly	dghīya	دغية
quiet	mhedden	مهدن
to quit	wqef	وقف

R

rabbit	qniya	قنية
racism	'unṣurīya	عنصرية
racquet	rakīta	ركيتة
radiator	radyatur	ردياتور
radio	rādyū	راديو
railway station	mheṭṭa dyal tran	محطة ديال التران
rain	shta	شتا
rare	qlīlia	قليلة
rash	hbūb	حبوب
rat	ṭōbba	طوبة
raw	khḍer	خضر
razor	zezwar	زيزوار
razor blades	rizwan	رزوان

Q

DICTIONARY

to read	qra	قراء
ready	mūzhūd	موجود
reason	sabab	سبب
receipt	faktūra	فكتورة
receive	tweṣṣel	توصل
recent	zhdīd	جديد
recognise	ʿref	عرف
recommend	nṣeh	نصح
recording	tszhīl	تسجيل
recycling	tzhdīd	تجديد
red	hmer	حمر
referee	hakam	حكم
reference	dalīl	دليل
refrigerator	tellazha	تلاجة
to refund	ʿuwwed	عوض
to refuse	rfeḍ	رفض
region	nahīya	ناحية
to regret	ndem	ندم
relationship	ʿalaqa	علاقة
relax	starah	ستارح
religion	dīn	دين
religious	dīnī	ديني
remember	ʿqel ʿla	عقل علي
remote	munʿazil	منعزل
to rent	kra	كراء
to repair	ṣlah	صلح
to repeat	awed	عاود
ruins	atar	اتار
rules	qawanīn	قوانين
to run	zhra	جرا

S

sad	mqelleq	مقلق
safe (adj)	salma	سالمة
safe (n)	khzana	خزانة
salad	shlada	شلادة
salary	'uzhra	اجرة
salt	melha	ملح
same	bhal bhal	بحال بحال
sand	remla	رملة
sandal	sandala	صندلة
sandwich	kaskrūt	كاسكروت
sanitary napkins	fōṭa dyal lhīd	فوطة ديال الحيض
Saturday	ssebt	سبت
sausage	sūsīs	سوسيس
save	sellek	سلك
say	gal	قال
to scale	tleʿ	طلع
scared	khayf	خايف
scenery	menḍer	منظر
school	medrāsa	مدرسة
science	ʿulum	علوم
scientist	'ilmī	عالم
scissors	meqqes	مقص
to score	hsab	حساب
screw	vīs	فيس
screwdriver	tūrnūvīs	طرنفيس
sea	bher	بحر
seasick	ddūkha dyal lbher	دوخة ديال البحر
seaside	shaṭī	شطي
seat	kursī	كرسي
seatbelt	ṣemṭaī	صمطة
second	tanī	تاني
second (time)	tanīya	تانية
secretary	sukritīra	سكرتيرة
see	shaf	شاف
self-service	tserbī raṣek	تسربي راسك
sell	baʿ	باع
send	ṣeifeṭ	سفط
sensible	mʿqōl	معقول
sentence (words)	zhūmla	جملة
sentence (prison)	thkīm	تحكم
to separate	ferreQ	فرق
series	halaqat	حلقات
service	serbīs	سربيس
sew	kheyyeṭ	خيط
shade	ḍell	ضل
shampoo	shampwan	شامبوان
shape	fōrma	فورمة
share (with)	ferreq	فرق
shave to	hessen	حسن
she	hiya	هي

sheep	hawlī	حاولي
sheet (bed)	īzar	ليزار
sheet (of paper)	werqa	ورقه
shelves	mrafeᶜ	مرافع
ship	babūr	بابور
to ship	Sīft ᶜala lbahr	صفت علي البحر
shirt	qamīzha	قاميسة
shoe lace	sīr	سير
shoe shop	hanūt dyal ṣṣebbaṭ	حانوت ديال صباط
shoes	ṣebbaṭ	صباط
shop	hanūt	حانوت
to shop	tqeḍḍa	تقد
short	qṣeir	قصير
shortage	naqs	نقص
shorts	shōrt	شورت
shoulder	ktef	كتاف
to shout	ghowwet	غوت
to show	werra	وري
shower	dūsh	دوش
shrine	muqeddes	مقدس
shut (adj)	msdūd	مسدود
to shut	sedd	سد
shy	heshman	حشمان
sick	mrīḍ	مريض
sickness	merḍa	مرض
side	zhenb	جنب
signature	tawqīᶜ	توقيع
silver	neqra	نكر
similar	bhal bhal	بحال بحال
simple	ᶜadī	عادي
sing	ghenna	غني
singer	mughannī	مغني
single (person)	ᶜazrī	عزري
single room	bīt dyal wahed	بيت ديال واحد
sister	khet	اخت
to sit	gles	كلس
Sit down! gles!		كلس
size	qyas	قياس
to ski	tzhleq	تزلق

skin	zheld	جلد
sky	sma	سماء
sleep	nᶜsa	نعس
sleepy	fīh nnᶜas	فيه النعاس
Slow down! beshwīya ᶜlīk!		بشوي عليك
slow	beshwīya	بشوي
slowly	beshwīya	بشوي
small	ṣghīr	صغير
smell	rīha	ريحة
to smell	shemm	شم
to smile	tbessem	تبسم
smoke (n)	dukhkhan	دخان
smoke a cigarette	kma	كما
snake	hensh	حنش
snow	telzh	تلج
soap	ṣābūn	صابون
soccer	kōra	كرة
socks	tqasher	تقاشر
soft	rṭeb	رطب
soft drink	munāḍa	موناضة
solid	qaṣeh	قاصح
some	shī	شي
somebody	shī wahed	شي واحد
something	shī hzha	شي حاجة
sometimes	băᶜḍlmerrat	بعض المرات
son	weld	ولد
song	aghniyya	اغنية
soon	deghīya	دغيا
sound	ṣōt	صوت
sour (unseasoned)	mssūs	مسوس
south	zhanūb	جنوب
space	tīsaᶜ	تيساع
speak	tkellem	تكلم
special	khaṣṣ	خاص
specialist	mukhtaṣ	مختص
speed	surᶜa	سرعة
speed limit	hedd ssurᶜa	حد السرعة
spend the night	bat	بات
spicy (hot)	har	حار
spoon	mᶜelqa	معلقة
sport	rīyaḍa	رياضة

sprain	fdeᶜ	فدع
spring (season)	rbīᶜ	ربيع
square (in town)	saha	ساحة
stadium	tīran	تيران
stairs	drūzh	دروج
stale	qdīm	قديم
stamp	tanber	تنبر
standard (usual)	'adī	عادي
star	nezhma	نجمة
to start	bda	بدأ
station	mheṭṭa	محطة
stay	bqa	بقي
to steal	sreq	سرق
steam	bukhar	بخار
steep	waqef	واقف
stomach	kersh	كرش
stone	hezhra	حجرة
stop light	ḍu lhmer	ضو الاحمر
stop sign	sṭup	سطوب
Stop! weqef!		وقف!
storm	ᶜaṣīfa	عاصفة
story	qeṣṣa	قصة
stove	furnu	فورنو
straight	nīshan	نيشان
strange	fshīshkel	فشي شكل
stranger	ghrib	غريب
stream	wad	واد
street	zenqa	زنقة
strength	qowwa	قوة
strike	īḍrab	اضراب
string	kheyyet	خيط
to stroll	tsara	تصرة
strong	ṣhīh	شيح
stubborn	rasu qaseh	راسه كاسح
student	ṭālīb	طالب
stupid	mkellekh	مكلخ
suburb	hay	حي
success	nazhah	نجاح
suffer	t'ᶜaddeb	تعذب
sugar	sūkkar	سكر
suitcase	balīza	بليزة
summer	ssīf	صيف
sun	shems	شمس
sunglasses	nḍaḍer dyal shshems	نضاضر ديال شمس
sunny	mshemes	مشمس
sunrise	shruq dyal shshems	شروق ديال الشمس
sunset	ghrub dyal shshems	شروق ديال الشمس
sure	m'ekked	ماكد
surface mail	bared ᶜadī	بريد عادي
surprise	ᶜla ghifla	علي غفلة
sweater	trīkū	تريكو
sweet	hlew	حلو
sweets	helwat	حلوة
to swim	ᶜūm	عوم
swimming	ᶜuman	عومان
swimming pool	pīsīn	بيسين
swimsuit	hwayezh dyal lᶜuman	حوايج ديال العومان
sword	sīf	سيف
syringe	ībra	ابرة

T

T-shirt	tī shūrt	تي شرت
table	ṭābla	طابلة
tablet (medicine)	fanīda	فنيدة
tail	qezzība	قزيبة
tailor	kheyyaṭ	خياط
take (away)	dda	دي
to talk	tkellem	تكلم
tall	ṭwīl	طويل
tampons	zīf dyal ddemm	زيف ديال الدم
tape	skātsh	سكوتش
to taste	daq	داق
tasty	bnīna	بنينة
tax	ḍārība	ضريبة
taxi	ṭāksī	تكسي
taxi stand	blaṣa dyal taksī	بلاسة ديال التاكسي
tea	atei	اتاي
teacher	'ūstad	استاذ

teaching	tᶜlīm	تعليم
team	ferqa	فرقة
tear (crying)	demᶜa	دمعة
teeth	snan	سنان
telegram	tilīgram	تليكرام
telephone	telefun	تليفون
television	telfaza	تلفزة
to tell	gal	كال
temperature (fever)	skhana	سخانة
tennis	tīnīs	تنيس
tennis court	tīran dyal ttīnīs	تيران ديال التنيس
tent	gītūn	كيطون
tenth	ᶜasher	عاشر
terrible	khayb	خايب
test	imtīhan	امتحان
thank	shker	شكر
Thank you. shukran		شكرا
theatre	meṣreh	مسرح
they	huma	هما
thick	ghlīḍ	غليظ
thief	sheffer	شفار
thin	rqeiq	رقيق
thing	hazha	حاجة
think	fker	فكر
third	tulut	تولوت
thirst	ᶜṭesh	عطش
thirsty	ᶜăṭshan	عطشان
this (one)	hada	هدا
thought	tefkīr	تفكير
thread	kheyṭ	خيط
throat	helq	حلق
throw	lah	لاح
ticket	werqa	ورقة
tight	mzeyyer	مزير
time	weqt	وقت
tin (can)	huk	حق
tin opener	ssarūt	ساروت
tip (gratuity)	tedwira	تضويرة
tired	ᶜeyyan	عيان
tobacco	taba	طابة
tobacco kiosk	ṣaka	صاكة
today	lyūm	اليوم
together	mezhmuᶜin	مجموعين
toilet	bīt lma	بيت الماء
toilet paper	kaghit dyal bit lma	كاغيط ديال بيت الماء
tomorrow	ghedda	غدا
tongue	lsan	لسان
tonight	had llīla	هد الليلة
too (also)	hetta	حتي
too much	bezzaf	بزاف
tooth	senna	سنة
toothache	ṣda' dyal ssnan	صداع ديال السنان
toothbrush	shīṭa d ssnan	شيتة ده سنان
toothpaste	mᶜzhūn dyal ssnan	معجون ديال السنان
top	qīmma	قمة
torch	ppīl	بيل
to touch	qāṣ	قاس
tour	ṭzhwīsa	طجويصة
tourist	sa'īh	سايح
towel	fuṭa	فوطة
tower	ṣemᶜā	سمعة
town	mdīna	مدينة
to trade	tbadel	تبادل
traffic	zHam	زحام
train	tran	تران
train station	mhetta dyal tran	محطة ديال التران
translate	terzhem	ترجم
translation	terzhama	ترجمة
travel	ṣāfer	سافر
travel agency	mekteb 'asfar	مكتب السفر
travellers cheque	shek sīyahī	شيك سياحي
tree	shezhra	شجرة
trip	ṣefra	سفرة

trousers	serwel	سروال
truck	kamīyū	كاميو
true	haqīqī	حقيقي
trust	tīqa	ثقة
truth	huqq	حق
try	hawel	حاول
turn (n)	nūba	نوبة
Turn left. ḍōr ˁl līser		دور علي اليسار
Turn right. ḍōr ˁl līmen		دور علي اليمين
Turn! ḍur!		دور !
TV	telfaza	تلفزة
twice	zhuzh khṭrat	جوج خطرات
twins	twam	توام
to type	ḍreb ˁal daktīlū	ضرب علي الدكتيلو
tyres	bnuwat	بنوات

U

umbrella	mḍell	مضل
under	teht men	تحت من
understand	fhem	فهم
understood	mefhūm	مفهوم
unemployed	shumur	شمور
unemployment	shumazh	شماج
unions	itīhad	اتحاد
universe	kawn	كون
university	zhamīˁa	جامعة
unsafe	khaṭar	خطر
untie	hell	حل
until	hetta	حتي
unusual	ˁzhīb	عجيب
up	fuq	فوق
uphill	taleˁ	طالع
upset (mad)	mqelleq	مقلق
urgent	mezrub	مزروب
to use	steˁmel	ستعمل
useful	ṣalha	صالحة

V

vacant	khawī	خاوي
vacation	ˁutla	عطلة
vaccination	zhelba	جلبة
valley	wad	واد
valuable	ghalī	غالي
value (price)	qīma	قيمة
vase	mehbeq	محبق
vegetables	khḍra	خضرة
vegetarian	makayakūlsh lhem	مكا يكلش اللحم
vegetation	khuḍra	خضرة
vein	ˁerq	عرق
very	bezzaf	بزاف
video cassette	kassīt vidyu	كاسيط فيديو
view	menḍer	منضر
village	qerya	قرية
vine	ˁenba	عنبة
virus	zhartūma	جرتومة
visa	t'shīra	تأشيرة
to visit	zar	زار
vitamin	vītamīn	فيتامين
voice	ṣuṭ	صوت
to vomit	tqeyya	تقية
to vote	ṣowweṭ	صويت

W

to wait	tsenna	تسني
waiter	garsun	كارسون
to wake up	faq	فاق
to walk	temsha ˁla rezhlīn	تمشي علي الرجلين
wall	heyṭ	حيط
to want	bgha	بغي
war	harb	حرب
warm	dafī	دافي
warn	nebbeh	نبه
wash	ghsel	غسل
wash (clothes)	ṣebben	صبن

washing machine	makīna dyal ghsīl	مكينة ديال الغسيل
to watch	shaf	شاف
watch	magana	مكنة
Watch out! 'ndak!		عندك!
water	lma	الماء
waterfall	shllalat	شلالات
watermelon	dellah	دلاح
wave (ocean)	mūzha	موجة
way	ṭrīq	طريق
we	hna	حنا
weak	ḍ'īf	ضعيف
wealthy	ghanī	غني
to wear	lbes	لبس
weather	hal	حال
wedding	'ers	عرس
week	ssīmana	صيمنة
weekend	lkhīr dyal ṣīmana	اخرديال الصيمنة
weigh	'ber	عبر
weight	'bar	عبار
welcome	mrehba	مرحبا
well	bīr	بير
west	gherb	غرب
wet	fazeg	فازق
What? ashnū?		اشنو؟
wheel	rweiḍa	رويضة
wheelchair	kursī mutaharrik	كرسي متحرك
When? īmta?		امتي
Where? fīn?		فين
Which? ashmen?		اشمن ؟
white	byeḍ	بيض
Who? shkūn?		شكون ؟
whole	kamel	كامل
Why? 'lash?		علاش ؟
wide	wase''	واسع
wife	mra	مراة
wild animal	hayawan mutawahhesh	حيومتوحش
to win	rbeh	ربح
wind	rīh	ريح
window	sherzhem	شرجم
wine	shrab	شراب
wings	zhnah	جناح
winner	rabeh	رابح
winter	shṭa	شتا
wire	selk dyal ḍō	سلك ديال الضو
wise	me'qōl	معقول
to wish	tmenna	تمني
with	m'a	مع
within	dakhel	داخل
within an hour	men daba sa'a	من داب ساعة
without	bla	بلا
woman	mra	مرا
wonderful	'azhīb	عجيب
wood	'wad	عواد
woods (forest)	ghaba	غابة
wool	ṣuf	صوف
word	kelma	كلمة
to work	khdem	خدم
work	khedma	خدمة
work permit	rōkhṣa dyal khedma	رخصة ديال الخدمة
world	'alam	عالم
worms	dūd	دود
worried	mqelleq	مقلق
worth	qima	قيمة
wound	zherh	جرح
to write	kteb	كتب
writer	katib	كاتب
wrong	ghalaṭ	غلط

X

x-ray	rādyu	راديو

Y

year	ʿam	عام
yellow	ṣfer	صفر
yes	īyeh	ايه
yesterday	lbareh	البارح
yet	mazal	مازال
yoghurt	danūn	دانون
you	'nta	انت
young	ṣghīr	صغير
youth (collective)	shabab	شباب
youth hostel	dar shshabab	دار الشباب

Z

zipper	sensla	سنسلة
zoo	hadīqa delhayawa	حديقة دل حيوان

INDEX

INDEX

LONELY PLANET PHRASEBOOKS

Complete your travel experience with a Lonely Planet phrasebook. Developed for the independent traveller, the phrasebooks enable you to communicate confidently in any practical situation – and get to know the local people and their culture.

Skipping lengthy details on where to get your drycleaning ironed, information in the phrasebooks covers bargaining, customs and protocol, how to address people and introduce yourself, explanations of local ways of telling the time, dealing with bureaucracy and bargaining, plus plenty of ways to share your interests and learn from locals.

Arabic (Egyptian)
Arabic (Moroccan)
Australian
Introduction to Australian English, Aboriginal and Torres Strait languages
Baltic States
Covers Estonian, Latvian and Lithuanian
Bengali
Brazilian
Burmese
Cantonese
Central Asia
Central Europe
Covers Czech, French, German, Hungarian, Italian and Slovak
Eastern Europe
Covers Bulgarian, Czech, Hungarian, Polish, Romanian and Slovak.
Ethiopian (Amharic)
Fijian
French
German
Greek
Hill Tribes
Hindi/Urdu
Indonesian
Italian
Japanese
Korean
Lao
Malay
Mandarin
Mediterranean Europe
Covers Albanian, Croatian, Greek, Italian, Macedonian, Maltese, Serbian and Slovene
Mongolian
Nepali
Papua New Guinea (Pidgin)
Pilipino (Tagalog)
Quechua
Russian
Scandinavian Europe
Covers Danish, Finnish, Icelandic, Norwegian and Swedish
South-East Asia
Covers Burmese, Indonesian, Khmer, Lao, Malay, Tagalog (Pilipino), Thai and Vietnamese
Spanish (Castilian)
Also Includes Basque, Catalan and Galician
Spanish (Latin American)
Sri Lanka
Swahili
Thai
Tibetan
Turkish
Ukrainian
USA
Introduction to US English, Vernacular, Native American languages and Hawaiian
Vietnamese
Western Europe
Useful words and phrases in Basque, Catalan, Dutch, French, German, Greek, Irish, Italian, Portuguese, Scottish Gaelic, Spanish (Castilian) and Welsh

COMPLETE LIST OF LONELY PLANET BOOKS

AFRICA

Africa - the South • Africa on a shoestring • Arabic (Moroccan) phrasebook • Cairo • Cape Town • Central Africa • East Africa • Egypt • Egypt travel atlas • Ethiopian (Amharic) phrasebook • The Gambia & Sengal • Kenya • Kenya travel atlas • Malawi, Mozambique & Zambia • Morocco • North Africa • South Africa, Lesotho & Swaziland • South Africa, Lesotho & Swaziland travel atlas • Swahili phrasebook • Tunisia • Trekking in East Africa• West Africa • Zimbabwe, Botswana & Namibia • Zimbabwe, Botswana & Namibia travel atlas

Travel Literature: The Rainbird: A Central African Journey • Mali Blues • Songs to an African Sunset: A Zimbabwean Story

ANTARCTICA

Antarctica

AUSTRALIA & THE PACIFIC

Australia • Australian phrasebook • Bushwalking in Australia • Bushwalking in Papua New Guinea • Fiji • Fijian phrasebook • Islands of Australia's Great Barrier Reef • Melbourne • Micronesia • New Caledonia • New South Wales • New Zealand • Northern Territory • Outback Australia • Papua New Guinea • Papua New Guinea phrasebook • Queensland • Rarotonga & the Cook Islands • Samoa • Solomon Islands • South Australia • Sydney • Tahiti & French Polynesia • Tasmania • Tonga • Tramping in New Zealand • Vanuatu • Victoria • Western Australia

Travel Literature: Islands in the Clouds • Sean & David's Long Drive

CENTRAL AMERICA & THE CARIBBEAN

Bahamas, Turks & Caicos • Bermuda • Central America on a shoestring • Costa Rica • Cuba • Eastern Caribbean • Guatemala, Belize & Yucatán: La Ruta Maya • Jamaica • Panama

Travel Literature: Green Dreams: Travels in Central America

EUROPE

Amsterdam • Andalucia • Austria • Baltics States phrasebook • Berlin • Britain • Canary Islands • Central Europe on a shoestring • Central Europe phrasebook • Czech & Slovak Republics • Denmark • Dublin • Eastern Europe on a shoestring • Eastern Europe phrasebook • Estonia, Latvia & Lithuania • Europe • Finland • France • French phrasebook • Germany • German phrasebook • Greece • Greek phrasebook • Hungary • Iceland, Greenland & the Faroe Islands • Ireland • Italian phrasebook • Italy • Lisbon • London • Mediterranean Europe on a shoestring • Mediterranean Europe phrasebook • Paris • Poland • Portugal • Portugal travel atlas • Prague • Romania & Moldova • Russia, Ukraine & Belarus • Russian phrasebook • Scandinavian & Baltic Europe on a shoestring • Scandinavian Europe phrasebook • Slovenia • Spain • Spanish phrasebook • St Petersburg • Switzerland • Trekking in Spain • Ukrainian phrasebook • Vienna • Walking in Britain • Walking in Italy • Walking in Switzerland • Western Europe on a shoestring • Western Europe phrasebook

Travel Literature: The Olive Grove: Travels in Greece

INDIAN SUBCONTINENT

Bangladesh • Bengali phrasebook • Bhutan • Delhi • Goa • Hindi/Urdu phrasebook • India • India & Bangladesh travel atlas • Indian Himalaya • Karakoram Highway • Nepal • Nepali phrasebook • Pakistan • Rajasthan • South India • Sri Lanka • Sri Lanka phrasebook • Trekking in the Indian Himalaya • Trekking in the Karakoram & Hindukush • Trekking in the Nepal Himalaya

Travel Literature: In Rajasthan • Shopping for Buddhas

COMPLETE LIST OF LONELY PLANET BOOKS

ISLANDS OF THE INDIAN OCEAN
Madagascar & Comoros • Maldives • Mauritius, Réunion & Seychelles

NORTH AMERICA
Alaska • Backpacking in Alaska • Baja California • California & Nevada • Canada • Chicago • Deep South • Florida • Hawaii • Honolulu • Los Angeles • Mexico • Mexico City • Miami • New England • New Orleans • New York City • New York, New Jersey & Pennsylvania • Pacific Northwest USA • Rocky Mountain States • San Francisco • Seattle • South-West China • Southwest USA • USA phrasebook • Washington, DC & the Capital Region
Travel Literature: Drive thru America

NORTH-EAST ASIA
Beijing • Bhutan • Cantonese phrasebook • China • Hong Kong • Hong Kong, Macau & Guangzhou • Japan • Japanese phrasebook • Japanese audio pack • Korea • Korean phrasebook • Kyoto • Mandarin phrasebook • Mongolia • Mongolian phrasebook • North-East Asia on a shoestring • Seoul • South -west China • Taiwan • Tibet • Tibet phrasebook • Tokyo
Travel Literature: Lost Japan

MIDDLE EAST & CENTRAL ASIA
Arab Gulf States • Arabic (Egyptian) phrasebook • Cairo • Central Asia • Central Asia phrasebook • Iran • Israel & the Palestinian Territories • Israel & the Palestinian Territories travel atlas • Istanbul • Jerusalem • Jordan & Syria • Jordan, Syria & Lebanon travel atlas • Lebanon • Middle East • Turkey • Turkish phrasebook • Turkey travel atlas • Yemen
Travel Literature: The Gates of Damascus • Kingdom of the Film Stars: Journey into Jordan

SOUTH AMERICA
Argentina, Uruguay & Paraguay • Bolivia • Brazil • Brazilian phrasebook • Buenos Aires • Chile & Easter Island • Chile & Easter Island travel atlas • Colombia • Ecuador & the Galápagos Islands • Latin American Spanish phrasebook • Peru • Quechua phrasebook • Rio de Janeiro • South America on a shoestring • Trekking in the Patagonian Andes • Venezuela
Travel Literature: Full Circle: A South American Journey

SOUTH-EAST ASIA
Bali & Lombok • Bangkok • Burmese phrasebook• Cambodia • Ho Chi Minh City • Indonesia • Indonesian phrasebook • Indonesian audio pack • Jakarta • Java • Kyoto • Laos • Laos travel atlas • Lao phrasebook • Malay phrasebook • Malaysia, Singapore & Brunei • Myanmar (Burma) • Philippines • Pilipino phrasebook • Singapore• South-East Asia on a shoestring • South-East Asia phrasebook • Thailand • Thailand's Islands & Beaches • Thailand travel atlas • Thai phrasebook • Thai Hill Tribes phrasebook • Thai audio pack • Vietnam • Vietnamese phrasebook • Vietnam travel atlas

ALSO AVAILABLE: Brief Encounters • Not the Only Planet• Travel with Children •Traveller's Tales

For ordering information contact your nearest Lonely Planet office.

PLANET TALK

Lonely Planet's FREE quarterly newsletter

Every issue is packed with up-to-date travel news and advice including:

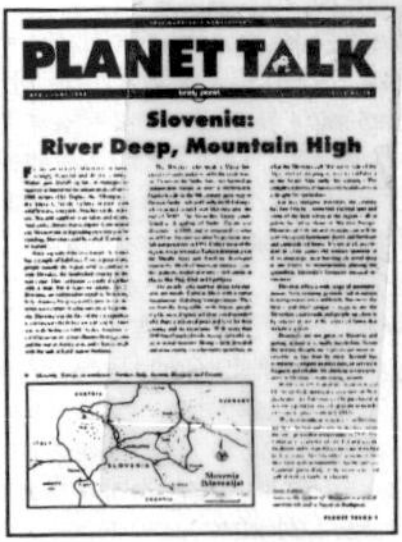

- a letter from Lonely Planet co-founders Tony and Maureen Wheeler
- go behind the scenes on the road with a Lonely Planet author
- feature article on an important and topical travel issue
- a selection of recent letters from travellers
- details on forthcoming Lonely Planet promotions
- complete list of Lonely Planet products

To join our mailing list contact any Lonely Planet office.

LONELY PLANET PUBLICATIONS

AUSTRALIA
PO Box 617, Hawthorn 3122, Victoria
tel: (03) 9819 1877 fax: (03) 9819 6459
e-mail: talk2us@lonelyplanet.com.au

USA
150 Linden Street,
Oakland, CA 94607
tel: (510) 893 8555
TOLL FREE: 800 275-8555
fax: (510) 893 8572
e-mail: info@lonelyplanet.com

UK
10a Spring Place,
London NW5 3BH
tel: (0171) 428 2800 fax: (0171) 428 4828
e-mail: go@lonelyplanet.co.uk

FRANCE:
1 rue du Dahomey, 75011 Paris, France
tel: 01 55 25 33 00 fax: 01 55 25 33 01
e-mail: bip@lonelyplanet.fr

World Wide Web: http://www.lonelyplanet.com
or AOL keyword: lp